Bachelor of Divinity

UNCERTAIN SERVANTS IN
SEMINARY AND MINISTRY

UNCERTAIN SERVANTS
IN SEMINARY AND MINISTRY

Bachelor of Divinity

By WALTER D. WAGONER

with drawings by JAMES CRANE

ASSOCIATION PRESS   New York

Publisher's stock number: 1521
Library of Congress catalog card number: 63-16044
72

Printed in the United States of America

FOR

SIDNEY LOVETT

CHAPLAIN EMERITUS, YALE UNIVERSITY

He set the standards

CONTENTS

7

A PERSONAL PREFACE:
FROM THE SEMINARY STEPS

There are some 20,000 students preparing for church careers in the accredited Protestant seminaries of the United States and Canada. This book is the result of an invitation by the officers of the Interseminary Movement, in co-operation with Association Press, to put on paper a series of essays and observations regarding the general health and body tone of this group of students, in the first place, and, in the second place, observations concerning theological education and the ministry.

What we have here—and no more is promised—is a walking tour through the countryside of theological education, with Baedeker commentary on this or that aspect of the landscape. No definitiveness or formal unity is attempted. Further, the guided tour ends with "A Personal Postscript: Ordination and Authority," which differs from the rest of the book. It presents without equivocation a personal viewpoint, not a sampling or a description of trends. This postscript is, alas, probably a minority report, but I am convinced that the issues raised are valid; and that the seminarian who does not think through these issues *before* ordination is going to have a shaky time of it. The section contains a bit of ecclesiology with which some of the tourists may grow restless. But, as with a tour of the United Nations or the Louvre, you are "asked to stay with your guide the whole way."

Each generation of seminarians and younger ministers has its peculiar configurations of hopes and fears, in addition to the recurring patterns of seminary life and thought. The items pointed to in this book were not the result of decisions made by pollsters or graph paper. There is no claim to describe the "average" seminarian. What has been done is to put a wet finger in the wind on this seminary campus and that. Such impressions are not superficial; they have been collated with the unique experience of administering for eight years three very significant fellowship programs of The Fund for Theological Education: The Rockefeller Brothers Theological Fellowship Program, The Rockefeller Doctoral Fellowships in Religion, The Protestant Fellowship Program. These programs and collateral activities have made available to me a staggering amount of empirical evidence concerning what is going on in theological education, the younger clergy, and the church.

I react with a shudder to most of the paternalistic and earnest advice so often directed at "young men preparing for the ministry," as if they were lower form boys at a spiritual prep school. Benign advice, looking down the

long nose of experience, is a terrible bore. Hazlitt's warn-
ing that "we as often repent the good we have done as the
ill" is very much in order when it comes to books about
the ministry. Writing for and about seminarians has been
too much smothered in an unctuous, if cheerful, sentimentality.

Vocational self-consciousness can reach sickening dimensions, after which the symptom is nausea rather than
health. The physician who spends more time pondering
what it is *to be* a physician than on the practice and study
of medicine soon becomes a burden to himself and an embarrassment to the more competent of his colleagues, who
got that way by working at their craft rather than by gazing
excessively into the mirror. The seminarian and/or minister who broods for hours about role, status, image, and
relevance, with his soul like an open sore, is going to have
precious little time and energy left with which to witness
to the gospel. Wry honesty, if not downright disgust, cause
more and more to suspect that the ministry is "the tender-
est profession"—measured in terms of an almost paralyzing
self-consciousness. The ordained Christian ministry, by
way of partial excuse, is inevitably conducive to introspection. Only the sentimentally committed and the bovine can
chew their vocational cud forever without pausing to
think. The inner turmoil of faith and Christ's ever-disturb-
ing presence bring constant self-examination. For the
minister who must make a professional career out of discipleship there had better be moments of deep questioning. Likewise, the thoughtful seminarian, as with a man
contemplating marriage, ought to think about himself and
his faith—especially since the seminarian's bride is a great
deal less tangible.

As a boy I played a game of "Uncle Wiggly," in which the eager rabbit moved square by square according to the count of the spinner from the cabbage patch to the brier patch. He was forever landing on a square which read, "Go back five spaces to avoid Brer Fox," or "Miss a turn, hit by Farmer Jones's buckshot." The course of the modern seminarian and younger clergy runs no more surely. Today it may be that he will miss a turn because the Jesus of History and the Christ of Faith don't seem to be one and the same. Tomorrow it may be back five spaces because six sociologists growled at the Bourgeois, Middle-Class Church. Yesterday he never did leave the cabbage patch because of fear of the Giant Laity. And one time the game broke up in panic when he drew a penalty card which read, "You don't know Who You Are. Stay in your hole!"

This situation is certainly no game; and the issues cannot be laughed away. The ground over which the contemporary seminarian or younger clergyman takes his pilgrimage is an extremely rugged one. One can have only admiration for the ability of so many students to keep steadily on their way: existentialism on all sides, Tillichian ontology above, Bultmannian hermeneutics below, the surgical analysis of the church from all quarters, the eschatology of Schweitzer, the dogmatics of Barth, the unnerving demands of Bonhoeffer and Kierkegaard, the radical skepticism of linguistic analysis, the uneasy confusions deriving from all the slippery talk about "myth, symbol, and historicity," the challenge of ecumenicity to familiar and comfortable vocational postures—and all in an ethos of international chaos without and Freudian complexity within. We should not be surprised if seminarians waver and wander in the teeth of unrelenting gales, creating a pilgrim mood that oscillates between panic and promise.

The list of obstacles facing these men and women could be expanded to read like a roll call of the thousands of Amorites opposing the hundreds of Joshua. The issues are real; the intellectual challenges as impressive as they are engrossing. These challenges are not an excuse for whining. And I only wish that so many did not find them an excuse for running away.

Furthermore, the church is going to be crippled severely if the better seminarians walk out. The quality and strength of those preparing for the ordained ministry is one of the most significant of all indices by which to measure the vigor and the future of the Christian church. Thus, all involved in the enterprise of theological education need to keep talking and thinking about the nature of the ordained ministry and the best way to prepare for it. Just as Bachelor of Divinity succeeds Bachelor of Arts, it follows that able men and women will not attend seminaries where the educational task is seen as a mere honing of intellectual knives or as dormitories where one passes a few days between long week ends of field work.

The drawings by James Crane not only give additional depth and vision to this book: they testify to the enormous service which this type of artist can bring to the church. Quoting from Mr. Crane himself:

Humor is never lacking in a profound seriousness toward life, and those who would protect themselves from the possibility of the tragic by repressing its expression also eliminate the possibility of meaningful humor ... for me [the cartoon] is more often than not a defensive weapon—and a pretty feeble one at that—for protecting the little scrap of human integrity left in the threatened, frightened, heroically unheroic human person of our time.* [1]

And now, before beginning this casual tour, the author-guide would quickly and gratefully acknowledge his enormous indebtedness to his colleagues and friends associated with The Fund for Theological Education, particularly Nathan M. Pusey, Henry P. Van Dusen, Charles Taylor, Yorke Allen, Jr., and C. Shelby Rooks. Those who have added their strength to my weakness by criticizing unmercifully the manuscript of this volume are John Oliver Nelson, Keith R. Bridston, Finley Eversole, Theodore Bachman, and James Rietmulder.

WALTER D. WAGONER
Princeton, New Jersey

* All *numbered* notes are found under "Notes" at rear of book.

I. Two Cheers for the Parish

We shall have to take a look at "... modern man's unhappy love for the Church," his overwhelming desire for saving and sheltering truth, his yearning which, though posing as mockery and scorn, is still recognizable as disappointed hate-love. Indeed, while keeping in mind the hosts of people who, in this strange century of ours, flock in thousands to the "Kirchentagen," we cannot for a moment be unaware how exposed and vulnerable from every side the minister's life must seem, set as it is in the midst of a welter of ideological odds-and-ends, and faced with the totalitarianism and nihilism of the Atomic Age ... to choose this profession involves in some way or another choosing to man the outpost, and so choosing an unequalled danger which threatens, not only from without, but also and mainly from within.*

* Heinrich Vogel, *Consider Your Calling* (Edinburgh: Oliver and Boyd, Ltd., 1962), pp. 4-5. Used by permission.

1.

SOCIOLOGICAL THUNDER AND
CULTURAL LIGHTNING

One of the most perplexing and yet profound questions confronting the theological student, theological administrator, and bishop alike is the recent, yet consistent, trend of men deviating from the parish ministry. . . . The temptation arises at this point to lay the burden of the existent situation squarely on the shoulders of three obvious participants: the Institutional Church, the nature of the theological discipline itself, or the seemingly apparent cleavage between the two, which is a point of frustration for both.[1]

Those words were written by the chairman of the Duke University Divinity School Student Government in announcing an essay contest and community forum on this problem. Criticism of the whole structure and form of the Christian enterprise has reached such proportions on semi-

17

nary campuses that one would suspect, if the church were unionized, that a general strike was about to be called. More than criticism, the mood spills over into petulance, and now and then comes close to self-hatred and other curious perversities.

The church is accustomed to being criticized and reformed by its members. Yet it remains conservative enough to make a quick or radical response unlikely. But, like subterranean tremors presaging an earthquake, there are many warnings which suggest basic reconsideration of the usual forms of ministry and ecclesiastical organization. And mostly at the parish level. Two cheers are as much enthusiasm as can be mustered these days when seminarians analyze the cozy organizational habits of the church in grassy green suburbia or macadamized metropolis. These seismographic tremblings are, if anything, stronger in Europe and England than in the United States. We in this country are shored up by wealth, numbers, cultural empathies *and* by genuine congregational strength in a way not so typical of Europe. But the earthquake is coming.

One poll we should like to have taken in connection with this book would be "The ten writers who most influenced your seminary development." It is a sound bet that such a list would include at least two of the sociologists of religion: writers such as Herberg, Lenski, Winter, and Berger. By any intellectual litmus test, this school of writing has a powerful influence on most of contemporary seminarians. Closely related to them is the "Gray Flannel-Suburban-Status Seeking" genre of books, flowing acidly from the pens of a Vance Packard, Daniel Boorstin, and others who collect white collars like Davy Crockett after bounty-bearing raccoons. These books are well written and wittily popular;

and they coincide with a widespread interest among college-educated Americans in cultural narcissism.

What seminarian, what clergyman has not read a handful of these books and then turned to that introspection which tries to relate the sociology of the barbecue pit to the *koinonia* of the Lord's Supper? The intellectual is a natural foe of anything bourgeois; the Christian intellectual-cum-prophet positively salivates at an opportunity to browbeat the Main Street Philistines. This type of social criticism becomes an unthinking reflex action, so that practically no contemporary theologian can put pen to paper without sneaking in a sentence such as "... the Christian ministry is doomed to disappear with the bourgeois culture that made room for it." [2]

A reading of contemporary sociology of religion, popular to the point of surfeit among trembling seminarians, is a maddening experience. Maddening in the same way that Freud is: too much truth for comfort and too much overstatement. Sentences like the following are found in enough abundance to wallpaper a chapel:

> Seminaries for the training of religious functionaries, with some noteworthy exceptions, are frankly "professional schools" ... which simply means that they train their students how to operate effectively within the religious institution, with a minimum of intellectual preparation. Theology, at best, then becomes a professional ideology very much in the same way as some sort of patriotism is necessary for the professional soldier as a rationalization of his activity. [3]

Or this,

> Unless the evidence on human motives and actions accumulated by social psychology since William James can be dismissed

out of hand, we should certainly not be surprised if our ministers will generally become what the social situation expects of them—that is, become "successful" or, at the very least, strive toward this goal.[4]

And,

The pastor runs an ambulance service, so to speak—an important and indispensable aspect of the church's ministry; but his services in this respect are performed without ever contacting the powers that shape the destiny of the world and the metropolis. Religion is now relegated to the sphere of personal emotional adjustments.[5]

And,

. . . it is not difficult to see the current turn to religion and the church as, in part at least, a reflection of the growing other-directedness of our middle-class culture. The people in the suburbs want to feel psychologically secure, adjusted, at home in their environment; the very character structure that makes this so urgent a necessity for them also operates to meet the need. Being religious and joining a church is, under contemporary American conditions, a fundamental way of "adjusting" and "belonging"; through the built-in radar apparatus of other-direction it becomes almost as automatic as an obvious social requirement, like entertaining or culture.[6]

No wonder that Daniel Jenkins feels these books cause one to "almost reach the point of believing that the typical flourishing suburban church is, by definition, a conspiracy against God." [7] One very observant young minister, serving a parish in Chicago, has written the following parody:

THE BOX PEOPLE

That tribe known as the Box People has a long and distinguished history. No one is quite certain when the tribe began building their curious homes. . . . Generally, the floor is made of niceness, the walls of chumminess, and the roof is thatched over with rules. These homes are very secure against all invasions: the walls of chumminess keep unchummy people out, the roof of rules keeps God out, and the floor of niceness keeps everyone out—including the true selves of the Box People. The Box People call these structures "religions."

Some of you may have visited in one of these boxes. If you have, you will remember how safe and warm it was inside. When you looked up to see your God, it was comforting to see the rules to obey instead. When you looked sideways to see your neighbors, it was reassuring to see only chums. And when you looked down to see yourself, it was pleasing to observe only niceness.

Throughout their history, however, the Box People have had a recurring problem: while their "religions" are admirably constructed to keep God and man out, some flaw in the architecture makes the "religions" unable to keep people in. Down through the years there have been escapes from the boxes. These always disturb the Box People; it is quite disconcerting to them that some prefer the dangerous life on the outside.[8]

It is clever; it is penetrating; it reveals a good eye for shallowness. But how fair is it? Prophets, seeking justice, don't often worry about nicely balanced fairness. There is, nevertheless, a grim fascination in this type of writing. Like Greek tragedy, it produces a health-giving catharsis. But the total effect is misleading. These writings lead to clichés about human nature and the situation of the contemporary church. The redemptive realities present in the Church and in its ordained ministry deserve, not a less astringent, but a more accurate representation.[9] Kenneth Lynn has observed that this genre of writing produces pseudo-books.[10] All that one can say here is that sociologists, like all other men, labor within a limited perspective. Parenthetically, it ought to be noted that religious sociology at its best in American Protestantism is found in that group of scholars who have been close to the influence of the late H. Richard Niebuhr: Liston Pope, Kenneth Underwood, James Gustafson, and others. Theirs is a vein which more seminarians would do well to mine.

All this is by way of saying again that among seminarians and the younger clergy there is a profound unrest concerning the shape of the Christian church in our culture—a discontent which produces unceasing criticism, carping, and re-evaluation and, if the *Duke Divinity School Bulletin* be correct, a trend away from the parish ministry.

In a discussion with college seniors, President James McCord of Princeton Theological Seminary was asked why he thought there was so much devastating "picking on" the church in our society. Dr. McCord's reply was well taken: "What we are witnessing, I believe, is the final disestablishment of the church in the United States."

His implication was that although the church has been disestablished legally for more than one hundred fifty years, its snug "unofficial establishment" in our society is now coming to a painful close. The rattle heard is not that of death, but of an awkward and noisy readjustment of the church to a position of "aloneness" in American culture, no longer guaranteed an uncritical support by social folkways and mores. The seminarians know or sense this. Such a realization obviously causes a grating readjustment in their self-image as they circle round this cultural scene, uncertain whether they are witnessing cultic death or birth rites.

The question which hangs in the air over seminary talk

about this Christ-Culture dilemma is "Can the church be reformed before too much disillusionment sets in," or ". . . before a sizeable minority of the seminarians back entirely away from the ordained ministries?" "The summer is past, the harvest is over, the new Sunday school wing complete, the assistant ministers hired, the Bible group formed, and still we are not saved!" "Let those who will," say the students, "burn their church mortgages; we shall witness elsewhere."

In reality, the body tone of American Protestantism is not so sluggish as to deserve the diagnosis being accorded it by the sociological Jeremiahs or by the seminarians. The depth of the negative reactions takes more explaining. In addition to the obvious plight of the church in our culture as a cause for seminarian disenchantment we may be witnessing a situation comparable to the economic theory of marginal return. For at the same time as the church's cultural dilemma is pointed out so clearly, the size and institutional immensity of the church is beginning to have a palling effect. The multiplying agencies (the reality and symbol of which is "475 Riverside Drive" [11]), the routinization of charisma: all this causes for young and old alike a feeling of weariness, of dull duty and frustration. The French word *incivisme* best describes an observable mood of the younger churchmen. *Incivisme* is a sense of disenchantment, of disgust, of skepticism about the whole business of politics and bureaucracy. It leads to angular individualism and the revolt against authority, causing one to renounce the goals of large organizations.[12]

The understandable reaction of the younger generation is either a romantic (albeit desperately earnest) search for new forms of the church which can escape the dirtier fingers of culture, or a brittle negativism. In our kind of world the odds are stacked high against the ability of man to maintain his humanity, much less his Christian faith. Perhaps we shall see an outbreak of utopias or monasteries, despite what we Americans learned to our sorrow in the nineteenth century about Brook Farm. This time renewal and reform of the church must be fought out on culture's main battlegrounds—the arenas of big churches, big government, labor, cybernetics, overpopulation, and all the rest. If the seminarians and leaders of tomorrow's church retreat—in the name of misconceived "gimmicks" of church reform—then the church will lose the battle by engaging in rear-guard sniping actions.

William Clebsch, of the faculty of the Episcopal Seminary of the Southwest, poignantly described the old dilemma which now intrudes so painfully on the younger generation of the church. Referring to the fact that Marilyn Monroe's real name was Norma Jean Baker, he pointed out that Norma Jean Baker was killed by Marilyn Monroe, as person and *persona* fought it out in an identity crisis. So, too, he added, "Christian faith is always about to be murdered by its embodiment in Christian religion." [13]

A second cause for the vociferous dissatisfaction with the church *vis à vis* culture has a broader educational context: an issue which some social scientists consider the most baffling problem in education. It is the fact that each younger generation is separated from the assumptions of its older, parental generation by a distance which, for the first time in history, seems to be increasing geometrically. Previously the parental generation (in this case the older clergy and laity) could assume that the world into which the younger generation was being raised and educated would not be too

Incivisme—Interchurch Center

much different from its own. No more. The difference now widens explosively, with the result that the younger are more impatient and the older more baffled. The cultural situation of the church is probably understood by the young in a way which is now different almost in kind, rather than in degree.

If this is so, then the older generation will be advised not to throw at the present crop of seminarians such epithets and apostolic curses as "adolescent revolt," "Iconoclasts," or "Young Turks." These may miss the point, for the differences in outlook are in many cases much more profound.

One must say that the discontent of the younger group is close to real disloyalty, not in the sense of apostasy, but as a complete disavowal of almost everything which is conventionally "churchy." This critical group of seminarians is muttering, "Let's chuck it and look for something entirely different in the way of Christian community; and, if we can't find it or create it, let's crawl back into the landscape of humanity as laity, not as clergy."

It is against this background that the "Why I Quit the Ministry" syndrome must be understood—the incessant batting of one's head against the conventional forms of the church. Dean Pearson of Andover Newton Seminary sees the ultimate problem facing the seminarians:

Call the group what you will ... Christianity is impossible without a group. Decide that the present group is wicked, forsake it, gather another group ... and immediately you face the very same dilemma all over again.

It's a wise observation; but whether it will be heeded by those who have not had such experience themselves is doubtful. Maybe it is well that such advice should not serve as a brake on experimentation.

All this thunder and lightning has caused much new searching for new forms, a gratifying amount of dash and derring-do in inner city parishes, ecumenical study centers, lay retreats, Faith and Life Communities, and the like. There is an immediate need that all these gestures of creativity be examined and given a fair trial. Thus far, however, it is far from clear which will prevail and which direction the wistful pilgrims will go en masse.

Chicken and egg present their usual priority problem. Is it out of this radical dissatisfaction with the form of the organized church that there spin off centrifugally the combined protests and affirmations mentioned elsewhere in this volume: the lay movements and the nervous indecision about ordination and professionalization? Or, is the root cause an attrition of faith, defensively hidden by much talk about "church problems"? If the latter is one of the causes, the reconstruction of the church and the ordained ministry will little matter. The sheer volume of adverse criticism of the church does betray some failure of faith admixed with prophetic concern. When we lose faith in God we can still be perverse or nostalgic enough to cling to the church for a while. It is a terrible thing to lose God; being human, we find it hard to destroy or abandon at once his cult and his community. There is even a grain of enjoyment in getting others to join in the antiphon: "This was the House of God, let us whine and complain therein."

But let us hurry on and away from such suspicions. What shall those do whose adverse criticism of the church arises out of deep discipleship? Church history has in these found its reformers, if they are willing to match their eagerness to criticize with a willingness to carry a cross down the long, slow road of reform. Sheer intellectualized or passive avant-gardism will not do—though seminaries are replete with "espresso prophets." A recent cartoon portrays a bearded beatnik in his stained, turtle-neck sweater saying to his middle-aged wife, "I suddenly realized that I am an angry *old* man." That is the fate waiting just around the corner for all critics of the church who wish it cleansed but who don't want to put their own fingers in the suds. Those who will stay with this problem, working at it, proposing new alternatives, making mistakes, but doing all as men in love —it is to those that the fun and the joy belong.

2.

"Away, ye manicured deities of the suburbs," goes up the cry. "Press on to the inner city where Christ lies imprisoned in concrete! Westchester, Kenilworth, The Newtons: in the seminary lexicon these are synonymous with Sodom and Gomorrah. The golden calves, with commuting devotees, are stabled in Greenwich and Shaker Heights, Grosse Pointe and Princeton. Leave now behind the gods of Bel-Air and Monterey, follow the ark of the covenant to Harlem, to Hyde Park, to Hamtramack, to all the skid rows and brick jungles of America's creeping megalopolis!"

So the chorus emanating from seminary choirs, reading from scores by Bonhoeffer, Abbé Michenneaux, and Gibson Winter. In our day these seminarians and younger clergy are a hard-sell for soft church assignments.

Since urbanization is slowly swallowing us whole, we should be grateful enough for the peace corps movement of seminarians toward the inner city. The big city is undoubtedly the most pressing missionary challenge to the American churches, and it ought to enlist the energy and devotion of the scale which we as a nation put into foreign missions from 1830 to 1940.

The inner city certainly is more challenging to the seminarian than the suburb. Most seminary professors wave high this challenge. One is profoundly impressed by the student response and by the sacrifice and dedication involved in such a ministry.

The writing and the talk surrounding this challenge and response are, nevertheless, surfeited with clichéd judgments. The glib jargon needs to be criticized without, if we can, becoming defensive about the *status quo*. For there is a revolution on the parish doorstep.

There is so much aphoristic, half-truth talk about the inner city *vis à vis* the suburb that one pioneer of the inner city has said to seminarians doing field work in his parish, "The suburbs are as tough a place as the metropolis, and some of you, to listen to you, ought to do penance in the suburbs in order to expiate for the spiritual pride accrued while serving in the inner city." Meanwhile, the souls of the clergy out in Martini Heights reflect an undeserved amount of guilt feeling, as they sink beneath the salivation of the sociologists.

We are only now pulling our feet loose from those sticky labels and pejorative descriptions of "split-level parishes" and "crab-grass Christianity"—the whole Peter de Vries patois.[1] And loose, too, from the naïve assumption that the good guys and the bad guys are more easily labeled in the inner city than in suburbia. One suspects that the liberal Christian intellectual has a romantic mystique about the city these days—an inverted version of Thoreau—which somehow assumes that sin and grace are distributed in an uneven geographical spread.

What badly needs to be acknowledged is that even under the present types of parish structure any and all parishes present challenges; there are no sinecures for the conscientious pastor, either in the suburb or the city. As Gibson Winter himself puts it, "We must not ask what the metropolis is doing to our organizational enterprise but rather where and how we are called to serve, minister, and bear our testimony. Ministry, not survival, is our criterion." [2]

Elsewhere in this book, in the chapter on "The Relevance Syndrome," there are some observations concerning the new shape of the parish and the insistent demand for new forms of ministry. But some of the pressing issues are apt to be overlooked if people take rigid postures, polemically and self-righteously (as many seminarians do) for or against the various forms of parish structures we now have. There is work, discipleship, and satisfaction enough in any location. There are two issues obvious enough behind the smoke screen of all the present critique of suburb and inner city which ought to be identified. The first is the weakness of ethical humanism as a motive power for Christian service. The second is the way in which the clamor for new parish forms highlights the disordered logistics related to the distribution of the church's available manpower.

With regard to the first point, there is still, for all the theological revival, a non-Christian ethic of service animating many younger churchmen. "I am in seminary because of a desire to serve people and with only a hope of divine transcendence," is the way one seminarian phrased it. No one will argue with the good that these men may do, but there is this to be said to the most altruistic seminarian working in garbage-filled streets and with dope-filled gangs: namely, that the church never has endured, much less moved forward, on an ethic alone, despite the benefits to society of much nontheologically inspired goodness. Further, ethical individualism of this sort, though it may produce avant-garde experiments, easily tires, spawning unattached junior redeemers: working without benefit of the strategy and discipline of a faithful community. To this type of servant of the world's woes the church may doff its hat, even though it wishes such service could be sustained by theology and disciplined by the church.

All of which brings us to the second and more significant issue behind all the fuss about inner city and suburb: the symbolic difference between Horatio Alger and the Jesuits. American Protestantism is a blood relative of Horatio Alger: his individualism, his boot-strap egoism, his entrepreneurial religiosity. The Jesuits are a different breed: the command discipline, the evangelical phalanxes of the Lord, the follow-the-leader ethic. Yet Ignatius Loyola has this to ask of Horatio Alger: "In the face of rapidly modernizing society, the unsettling of formerly snug parish patterns, the growth of numbers, et cetera, et cetera, how is the available manpower of the church to be directed to areas of maximum need, whether in suburb, exurb, farmland, or metropolis, under your present system of manpower distribution?"

We may say that Loyola's legions have corrupted the answer; but our Protestant laissez-faire, Horatio Alger type of church polity is equally lacking. The complexities of suburb and city make it clear that most Protestant churches find and distribute manpower, often matching mice to mountains, in a nondisciplined manner which is just short of scandalous. This is true even of churches with episcopal polities.

The current stresses and strains on church resources and church organizational forms cannot be handled most advantageously in terms of catch-as-catch-can logistics. The growth of population, the mobility of church members, the onrush of urbanization: these demand a modification of the ways by which we now match men and women to the needs of the church.

In summary, the suburb-city debate needs to get away from clichéd talk about where the need is greatest or which is the easiest. The debate ought to be, within seminary and without, about what type of church polity is most adequate to matching peculiar ability with particular situation. And in this debate the old *jure divino* battle cries about polity are more sixteenth- and seventeenth-century echoes. The real issue is not whether presbyterianism, or episcopacy, or congregationalism represents the purest form of church polity but which of these (or some new combination) can handle the logistical job of the church. It seems likely that it will be a new combination.

To the seminarian, recently ordained and looking for a parish, the demand for a new polity based on disciplined obedience is a threat. It implies that a discipline of service is involved, a willingness to be "placed," and not simply,

Horatio Alger and the Jesuits

Horatio Alger fashion, a desire to go where he pleases—with the usual pulling of strings, oiling of machinery, and impressing of parish supply committees in order to get there. This manifesto for a new discipline in church logistics does not tickle our fancy. We Protestants are not quickly transformed from our self-images of heroic individualism, pulpiteer personalities and self-initiating job hunters to more pliable servants of the church's needs. The free-wheeling Protestant is almost unable to contemplate anything but a supply-and-demand system of auctioneering clergy-talent to the highest bidder. The Methodists, inheriting from John Wesley a precedent for placing clergy here and there, have the strongest tradition of episcopal control. In this respect even the Protestant Episcopal Church cannot match the Methodists. Nevertheless, neither the Methodist nor any other church can buck the auctioneering system very effectively. Further, to listen to Methodist ministers, their church has not solved the inevitable problems of lobbying, currying favors, winning over district superintendents and influencing bishops. At the other extreme, the presbyterian and congregational polities lack the sanctions for matching men, ability, and need. One of the back-room reasons for supporting the Blake-Pike proposals is the need to evolve a polity that will be able to deal more adequately with the manpower problems of the contemporary Protestant church. All who are concerned need to rethink our church polities. The era of church mergers is a propitious time for such thought.

The logistical imperatives challenging the church mean that an effective polity must include: (1) methods of knowing and assessing the abilities and weaknesses of the clergy and seminaries; (2) an updated knowledge of parishes, new frontiers of evangelism, church vacancies, and so on; (3) a regular review system of ministers in the field, their satisfactions and restlessness; (4) regional and national committees with authority to counsel and to implement. But listen to the shouts of horror! Dictatorship, bureaucracy, CCC camp ecclesiasticism! Well, the dangers are there. The larger question is that of comparative advantage. Will the machinery and the risks inherent in a more disciplined placement outweigh the obvious injustices of the present free-for-all? A very strong case can be made that our present methods are archaic and attended by grave injustice. There are also good grounds for believing that seminarians will recognize the merit in, even if they may not welcome, a more rigorous selection and assignment process.

Safeguards can be built into these strategies which will minimize autocratic corruption and hierarchical whimsy: review committees, consultation procedures, appeals, regular re-evaluations. More importantly, we shall need to reckon more honestly with salary structures. And now we invade the Holy of Holies of church placement systems! *The main trouble with clergy salaries is not that they are too low, but that they are not regularized.* We need—as in the French Reformed Church and as with colleges and universities—salary scales, salary ranks which apply across the board. By various formulas pegged to seniority, financial need, cost of living, and other facts, there ought to be five or six salary levels which apply to all clergy, whether in Greenwich Village or Greenwich, Connecticut. There are too many Fancy Dans in the clergy who seek other parishes primarily for monetary reasons. There are too many clergy who would like to stay where they are and who have stayed there at great sacrifice, but who, in order to educate their children and meet reasonable family living standards, *must* look to greener parishes. There are too many pastoral supply committees whose antics resemble nothing so much as football coaches bidding up the ante for two hundred fifty pound tackles. The first major denomination in the United States to establish stable and equitable financing for its clergy in such a way as *to remove the pay check as a primary reason for parish placement* will make a revolutionary contribution to Protestant church life. It can be done. Each local congregation, in proportion to its ability to pay, can earmark its salary funds to a national church treasury, something like present pension funds. Thus, the Rev. Mr. Jones of Wealthy Acres will get the same "fair" salary as the Rev. Mr. Smith of Slum Corners, assuming they have about the same seniority, family needs, and so on. If a particular church makes unusual financial demands upon its minister, it will be up to that church to furnish necessary expense funds. The proximate justice of this scheme is far greater than the rhymeless and reasonless present system. Specifically, the new clergyman in his first charge will begin with a base salary of, let us say, five or six thousand dollars, plus manse.[3] In the course of a forty-year career he will move toward a top of ten to twelve thousand dollars, plus manse. There are no more insuperable human or actuarial factors in such a scheme for the church than for the Civil Service or for the State University. Think what it would do, furthermore, to clear the air of all the ethical ambiguities now surrounding clergy recompense! Those arguments, analogies from the competitive free-enterprise system, about talent showing up in a free market of supply and demand, simply do not apply to the church. Nor is there any reason to believe that the Directors of the Salary Fund will arrogate Orwellian or paternalistic powers unto the denomination.

There is every reason for believing that such a salary plan would result in a more prophetic church, in clergy freer of the Damoclean financial sanctions of local congregations, and in seminarians more responsive to frontier posts. In this sense, such a salary proposal should be viewed as a major weapon in fighting for the spiritual integrity of the church and its clergy.

Under such a system, and with salary not a major item in decisions, John Jones of X Seminary decides that he will seek ordination. He then, sometime during his last year in seminary, submits his credentials (*vita*, academic achievement, testing, letters, interview evaluations, job preferences) to the appropriate assignment committee. Subject to examination and ordination, Mr. Jones is called before the committee to be asked his own desires. His desires can then be matched against the needs of the church—which have first priority. If desire and need correspond, fine; if not, Mr. Jones will be assigned to that position which the church feels most needs his talents.

On the other hand, Mr. Smith, pastor of Grover Corners for the last ten years, wishes a change of pace. He will have open to him effective, and not simply letterhead, channels of appeal and review.

The various sanctioning and decision-making committees will be made up of competent clergy and laymen, with a system of change and rotation which prevents cliques and nepotism.

Whatever the details, a challenge is now before the church: that somehow monetary incentive be reduced as a primary factor affecting the parish placement of ministers. At least as much thought should be devoted to this problem as is presently being given to the massive efforts to recruit and educate men for the ministry.

3.

ON BEING A
PROFESSIONAL CHRISTIAN

MY UNCLE, THE MONSIGNOR

My uncle Fitzpatrick, priest and Monsignor
splendid in robes of crimson and onyx,
laid his worn hands upon my head in benediction.

Remember, my son, you belong to God.
He has made you for Himself and will take you
to Himself. I would be happy to see you a priest.

Ours is not an easy life: the selfless giving
to all kinds of people; living in houses
devoid of comfort; avoiding idleness, luxury, ease,
learning to dine on the unostentatious
on moderate food and an adequate wine,
showing distaste for the rare vintage wine
for gooseliver paste and especially fine

imported caviar; consigning desires
to the will of God; praying always to do His will.

Pray for the grace to know your vocation,
for realization of what really matters;
I pray that you may be a priest.

Believe that God hears humble prayers.
Remember your uncle is a Monsignor.[1]

"Remember your uncle is a Monsignor." The poet not
only flails a self-conscious humility that preens itself on
getting ahead: he raises the whole issue of professionalism
in Christianity. H. L. Mencken put it more abrasively: "A
Bishop is a Christian who has achieved a higher ecclesiastical status than Jesus Christ!" Does God have hired men?
Well, in Kierkegaardian mood, there has probably never
been a seminarian or minister, Catholic or Protestant, who
has not pondered the question as to which is worse: to be
paid thirty pieces of silver to serve Christ, or to betray
Him? Those who hesitate at carrying a tax-deductible cross
are responding to a commendable instinct. And there is
plenty of such hesitation among seminarians and the clergy.
At pay-check time Christianity does seem to be a business.
We cannot escape such guilt feelings. We relish our ama-
teur standing in these matters. Why can't we just play on
Eton's fields rather than at Yankee Stadium? Paid discipleship carries overtones of sinecures and monetary motivation. Like the Christmas season, the faint odor of financial
prostitution mingles with the original incense. Who shall
deliver us from this financial bind? Even Billy Graham is
incorporated. It is a profoundly disturbing matter that witnessing to the gospel involves, to the seminarian looking

ahead and to the clergyman looking around, an unavoidable mixture of commercialization and personal faith.

As Dean John Coburn has accurately described it, the minister is "the man in the middle." [2] Not the midway position between God and Man, but as he personifies the paradox of being in but not of the world. He is midway, it often seems, between spontaneity and the duties of the pay check. Or, like the hired substitutes of the Civil War draft dodgers, his very professionalization makes of him a paid alter ego for the Christian community.

There are two current influences which make this dilemma a painful one for the seminarian. The first is that the great virtue of American culture is Individualism. Many are the Christian patriots who will justify Christianity because it protects individuality and individual rights. It is closer to the truth, however, to insist that the great Christian virtue is obedience. The two virtues do not always mix well, and the prominence of individuality in our scale of values in American culture makes professionalization (which at its best is a form of obedience) in Christian service a heavy burden to carry. Professionalization can thus appear to be a loss of individuality, of freedom, of laissez-faire discipleship; whereas professional obedience to Christ in the Church should be seen as one of the inevitable results of discipleship.

Another influence which puts professionalism in a poor light among seminarians and clergy is symbolized in the popularity of Bonhoeffer's writings about "religionless Christianity." The cultus of Christianity including the parish and preaching, is one among many forms of religion which need to be sloughed off, says Dietrich Bonhoeffer. He rejects a property-owning religious organization. From

St. Francis in the fields to Bonhoeffer in prison, it is obvious that such a critique is going to make the professional ministry seem an ill-fitting suit of clothes.

Further, the most casual glance outside seminary walls will reveal many types of professionalism. One of the least attractive is that "Christian Pro" who seems to have been so formed in the womb. "I like not," spewed Nietzsche, "these bugs who in their insatiable desire to smell of the Infinite make the Infinite smell of bugs." There are some professional Christians who appear to have graduated Magna Cum Odor from an assembly line for clergy and who go about "the Lord's work" with a brisk efficiency, operating out of the sales office in Jerusalem with never a sidelong glance at the Mount of Olives. Constant encounter with this crowd naturally turns halos into boomerangs and sends one to reading *The Way of All Flesh* during Lent.

A bothersome variant on the theme of professionalism—and one which is seen the more clearly by seminarians for being at a greater distance from it—is the financial favoritism shown to church and ministry: the clergy discounts, the manse (the church's own paternalism), the tax exemptions (does being legal make them ethical?), the fees for weddings and funerals, the dollars here and pennies there. The scrambling of dollar sign and cross is all too noticeable. If the seminarian can tighten his resolutions and principles before ordination, so much the better. If not, he may never see the awful humor reflected in a signboard outside a church: "The Rev. —————, the highest-paid clergyman in New England, will preach during Lent."

The face of professional Christianity is further and painfully reflected in the attitudes of those who seem most

sympathetically to surround the clergyman: the stereo-
typed responses which people make in the presence of the
ordained man, the shifts in conversation, the corny religious jokes, the awkward silences, the cloyed deference.
There is a dripping, Pavlovian piety here, a reflex action
to the clergyman's presence, which can be excruciating to
a sensitive pastor—and which parishioners reveal even before week-ending seminarians. This is a response which
most ministers do not deserve and certainly do not want.
It forces some to forego clerical garments or, in other ways,
to remain professionally incognito. The pathetic retreat
from such a situation is to overdo "being one of the boys."
The office of the ordained ministry does properly entail a
dignity, a visibility, an aloneness. One of the hallmarks of
faithfulness in the ministry is the willingness to endure
this aspect of professionalization. With humor, with perspective, and with good grace, it can and must be done.

One psychological albatross perching on the shoulders
of Christian professionals is the feeling of satiety which
now and again overwhelms, and which is most apparent
even to men just ordained. Day in, day out, religion, religion, religion. Contributed to by false distinctions between secular and sacred, compounded by the duties of
formal Christian observances, this mood needs safety valves
of vacations, a small group of friends among whom something other than theology is talked, a healthy variety of
secular activities. Living under the aspect of eternity is a
strenuous activity which can turn a conscientious Christian
into an existential brooding hen. For the professional
Christian it may lead also to that repulsive image of the
"man of God always smelling out some ultimate concern"
or, more likely, to a tiredness, a hidden hunger, a malnu-

Pavlovian Piety

trition due to a deficit of the juices and joys of ordinary human existence.

Thus, for these and so many other reasons, "religion is my occupation" is a phrase which for the sensitive seminarian and clergyman never quite loses its suspect overtones. He looks around him and finds that in the United States alone there are more than half a million persons for whom the organized Christian religion is the economic source of full-time employment, not to mention the printers, travel agents, hotel keepers, landlords, architects, and all the army of those who benefit economically on the side by the existence of the Christian church. The church is one of the wealthiest businesses and largest property owners in the land. There is no way to escape the fact that when one becomes a clergyman one sinks up to the hips in a vast economic and professionalized quicksand. The church is very much *in* the world; it is largely up to the clergy to use their very professional leverage as a means to making more certain that the church is not altogether *of* the world—to see that there are souls left for the heavily mortgaged mansions of the Lord. It is a challenge to the clergyman's integrity that his role as a religious professional makes it more difficult for him to be a true and faithful servant than to be a faithful Christian layman in secular society—a challenge to be welcomed.

Justice Brandeis defined a profession as "an occupation for which the necessary preliminary training is intellectual in character, involving knowledge and to some extent learning as distinguished from mere skill, which is pursued largely for others, and not merely for one's self, and in which the financial return is not the accepted measure of success." Or, as the cliché goes, the professional does not work in order to be paid; he is paid in order that he may work. One of the most competent social scientists has observed that "in no other occupation are so many different aspects of life bound together as objectives of [professional] training in the preparatory stages." [3]

Dr. Charles Taylor, Executive Secretary of the American Association of Theological Schools, in a helpful discussion of professionalism in the ministry,[4] cites the appeal of the worker-priest movement in France to those men who found in it not only a genuine demonstration of Christian service but also a means of avoiding middle-class professionalism— a ministry not vitiated by departure from the path and life of the common man. Some Roman Catholics found this movement distasteful, feeling that it sapped the uniqueness of the priesthood.[5] But those who see the ordained ministry as an office and not as an Order will want to avail themselves of every opportunity to identify themselves with the mainstream of human life. This instinct is quite noticeable among the present generation of seminarians. Dr. Taylor cites three reasons for valid professionalization: (1) to do that which no others do so clearly or so well, (2) to do it with a competence derived from special education, and (3) "to be a master of the art of living in which, he humbly recognizes, he has so much to learn from so many laymen." Underlining the second point is Taylor's quotation from Bishop Stephen Neill's book, *Anglicanism:*

Among the greatest achievements of the Council of Trent was its creation of the seminary. When the Protestants spoke bitterly of the returning emissaries of the Roman Church as "Seminary Priests," the name hit the mark; these young men, trained at Douai or elsewhere, had learned discipline and devotion; that they had been trained might be narrow and scholastic, but it was calculated to make them more than a match for anything that they were likely to meet in England.[6]

As an extenuating word on behalf of professionalization in Christianity, can it not be said that since it is apparently an economic and ecclesiastical necessity it need not be a major cause for stumbling? It is one of the tensions with which the church lives—from which it never escapes. All the timely warnings about clericalism, in-group righteousness, insularity, and so on cannot get around the fact that the church is a part of society. No Rousseauian gesture, no docetic impulse, will feed the clergyman and his family. The same budget that supports the work of the church in all its worship of God and service of men must include a paid ministry. Those who seek ordination must expect to wear this hair shirt without scratching in public.

Most significantly, a professional ministry *raises* the level and the effectiveness of the church—as the Society of Friends is just now finding out in the United States. The overview needs to take into account these words:

... they [professional people] need to protect themselves and defend their ideals; they need to understand and uphold their personal attainments . . . they are an aristocracy of a sort. They certainly need the humility which self-knowledge demands, and should discard the dangerous false modesty of pretending to be "ordinary people . . . only an expert in this or that." On the contrary it is important that their differences from other people should be emphasized; the atomic physicist is not an expert in the sense that a coal worker is an expert; nor are a doctor's or a lawyer's expertise, life, influence, and dignity comparable with those of a radio engineer or a packaging specialist. If so many activities must be professionalized—and there is no escape from that conclusion—let professional people emphasize the hierarchy of professions, of education, of esteem. Let them not shirk the truth expressed by Matthew Arnold: "the highly instructed few, and not the scantily instructed many, will ever be the organ to the human race of knowledge and truth. . . ." [7]

There is no surer way of nurturing heresy and obscurantism within Christianity than to abolish a paid, specially educated professional leadership. What other way is there to maintain this crucial cadre but by a seminary system of the highest order, which depends ultimately for its financial support upon the institution of the church? The ministry is no exception to all other areas of human progress and competence: without a skilled, professional leadership group, atrophy will set in. That much can be said to seminarians, can it not, without incurring the righteous wrath of those who are determined that grace not be confused with dollars, or discipleship with checking accounts? There is an entirely proper pride and esprit which ought to characterize members of one of the great and noble professions. If all the talk about false distinctions between clergy and laity tends to cheapen the standards of the professional ministry, we shall be victimized by poor logic. A vigorous and competent professional ministry is the right supplement to a strong laity.

4.

UNOFFICIAL HALOS:
SOME ENCHANTING LAYMEN

No more than 1 per cent of all Christians are ordained. Thus, the current stew and fuss about the revival and renewal of the laity seem curiously one-sided. There is a boom on in the laity; a phenomenon which to the older clergy must be an occasion for a chuckle. After all, the old-timers might well say, "With whom do you suppose we have been living and working all these years?" Nevertheless, the laity are the big thing. Seldom have so many clergy and theologians and seminarians and church boards and national conferences and ecclesiastical seances paid so much attention to the laity as today. To be a layman is very much O.K.; to be a clergyman is a very ordinary status. Within the last five years one publishing house alone has issued Hendrik Kraemer's theological analysis of the laity, Francis

Ayres' description of the ministry of the laity, and Arnold Come's abolition of them.[1] No self-respecting church or ecumenical organization is without its office suite dedicated to the laity. Not that they may not deserve it, but the laity have a mystique today in the eyes of the clergy which hasn't been rivaled since Queen Anne's touch.

What is afoot in this lay enchantment? Shall we, in the manner of a Mencken, cynically assume that the bill payers are being buttered? Is it a peasant's revolt of the button-down against the clerical collars? Or has some guilt laden administrator decided to atone for everything by sending out a directive entitled "Revive the Laity"? Flippancy may skirt the truth, but the fact of the matter is that all this genuine interest in the nature and role of the laity primarily derives from the renaissance of the theology and doctrine of the church.

It should not be overlooked either that much of this concentration on the laity is clergy sponsored. So much to the credit of the clergy and their enlightened self-interest —but the whole movement would look a great deal healthier if the laity themselves were the prime instigators. Apparently they are too busy just being laity.

Meanwhile, back in the seminary dormitories the pre-ordinands debate the virtues of lay and ministerial status. Their conversations betray a nervous earnestness, as if the words came from the lips of young ladies debating whether to surrender their virginity. Hanging in the air is the unspoken assumption that the laity are, by definition, in a purer state of grace. And, next to that, is the spoken assumption that most laymen are in a better position to advance the cause of Christ. Obviously, the themes of Christian professionalization and ordination are interwoven in these bull sessions.

The Rockefeller Brothers "trial-year" program is a showcase in this matter of lay-clerical tension. One of the central matters so many Fellows try to resolve is the comparative effectiveness of a lay versus a clerical witness. In most cases any given Fellow could do well in either category. The following lines are quoted anonymously from the report of a Fellow who finished his B.D. but then decided to go into the State Department in the hope that he would find a more effective milieu to witness more "naturally" to Christ. After two years of lay status, these were his words:

"I have found it quite exciting, but at present doubt that I will make government work a lifetime career. I still have a deep feeling for the pastoral ministry, and the same sensitivity toward the Church that I had when I first applied for a Rockefeller grant. Maybe I'm actually running away from it. I'm not quite as sure as I once was that one can do more in the type of position I now find myself than one can in the church. Maybe we have overemphasized the idea that the layman can have more influence than the professional religionist who is expected to say and do certain things, and who thereby supposedly loses his effectiveness. . . . some of us may be just plain afraid of the ministry."

It is an oft-repeated pattern.

The supposed bliss of the layman's status has likewise pulled many seminarians, not only Rockefeller Fellows, out of the Bachelor of Divinity route and toward the teaching profession, looking for a career in an undergraduate department of religion. Again, files are filled with letters of remarkable candor which say in effect: "Maybe I am afraid of the parish, but I can't figure out how to relate the gospel to a parish situation. Therefore, I am going to teach." Or, as one man said in his statement:

"What bothers me most about going into the parish ministry is my basically selfish desire to avoid, by going into college teaching, the difficult challenge of making the rudimentary duties of the ministry a meaningful part of my job. I would hope ultimately to overcome my reluctance to leave the academic community and to be able to put Christianity to work in the building committee, the evangelism program, the Community Chest drive, as well as in the spiritual lives of my congregation."

The moral of this quotation is not that teaching religion is the wrong career for many of these men—quite the contrary. Nor is it that all teachers of religion are refugees from the rigors of the parish—though many are so. The moral is that there is much romanticism abroad among seminarians and clergy concerning both the laity and the clergy and their degrees of effectiveness. At the moment the romanticism and naïveté surrounding the laity is much the thicker.

The worst possible face to put on the appeal of lay status to ambivalent seminarians is to hint that it may be a smoke screen for a lack of faith, a limping excuse to hide, rather than to witness, in the cavernous anonymity of the lay world. After all, a clergyman is identifiable as a Christian; his very office represents a public commitment. If a seminarian were to lose his nerve, looking forward to ordination, the least bothersome way out might be to say, *sotto voce,* "I have decided to remain a layman."

One slight indication of the favored-nation treatment now being given the laity is seen in the difference in style between anticlericalism and antilaitism. Among seminarians the worst and silliest types of clergy are great objects of scorn and buffoonery. Clergy are named and mercilessly scalped of their pretended halos. But seminarians and clergy, except in cases of intraparish squabbles, generally criticize the laity in the most general terminology, usually subsumed under a euphemism such as "the acculturized middle class," or "the sheep out in the pasture waiting to be pasteurized." The clergy are more sentimental in their judgments about the laity than vice versa. In either case, it is not an irenic scene.

A Protestant might well stare in horror, despite the delightful Protestant-Catholic camaraderie of Vatican Council II, at the sight of St. Peter's filled in plenary session with clergy, and only clergy, as far as the TV camera could see. It is nothing short of grotesque that the great deliberations of Roman Catholicism should be so clerical. But is Protestantism any better? The voting delegates to the Third Assembly of the World Council of Churches were 80 per cent clergy—and in a group where Roman Catholic assumptions about the nature of the church do not prevail. In the face of sights such as these many a sensitive seminarian wonders toward what type of clerical cultus he is heading.[2]

On the whole, and if the younger churchmen, both lay and clerical, are an indication, the laity of most Protestant churches can give thanks that so many future leaders of the church are bound and determined not to let the clergy "do it all." The rather awkward bowing and scraping between clergy and laity in these matters does, however, bring to mind the famous cartoon of James Thurber in which a *very* ordinary wife retorts to a *very* ordinary husband, "Well, I'm disenchanted with you, too." In such frank and mutual recognition lies the beginning of wisdom . . . and co-operation . . . and affection.

A fair interpretation of all the dust in the air these days on these matters is to recognize that in our wide-open culture the function of the ordained minister is not so neatly categorized as it once was. Consequently we have all the chatter about loss of role, status, function, image. Consequently there is a tendency to wear the incognito plumage of the layman. The less clear the definition of the ordained ministry, the greater the chances are that the seminarian considering ordination (or the college student considering seminary) will opt for the lay status.

More than that, the new breed of seminarian is increasingly acquainted with the frontiers of evangelism in politics, the arts, science, the mass media, and other areas; and feels that these frontiers can best be staked out by laity.

A portion of this ambivalence between ordination and lay status is incapable of diagnosis, of precise articulation —except, perhaps, by psychoanalysis. This is illustrated in the following paraphrase of an answer given by the admissions committee of an outstanding seminary to the question, "Why do some seminarians leave seminary?" After listing the expected—such as a sense of vocational unfitness, lack of money, domestic troubles, loss of faith, academic weakness—the committee went on to say: "On top of all that, we feel that the chaotic and unsettled state of the world, with so much going back and forth from nihilism to fanaticism, creates a deep inner restlessness which will not come to rest in the ordained ministry."

5.

THE RELEVANCE SYNDROME

Along with "encounter," "ontology," "existential," and "I-Thou," the word "relevance" is one of the shibboleths of the seminarian. "Is the church relevant?" "Is the ministry a relevant vocation?" These questions slouch toward bull sessions to be born. They are also among the most common, perhaps *the* most common, queries heard in interviews with candidates for the Rockefeller Brothers Theological Fellowships. If such anxiety is the smoke, what is the fire?

The fire seems to be a dread that the church and its ordained ministry have become marginal influences on men and society. The parable of the sower, even when remembered, doesn't dissuade the seminarians from brooding over their vocational impact, cutting edge, and relevance. Is the ministry but a vestigial remains of a once useful profession?

Hearing such complaints about relevance immediately tempts one to overwhelm the questioner with a show of superior moral force: "Did Jesus worry about relevance?" ... "Did the Cross seem relevant?" ... "Has the world ever paid real attention to these marginal people called Christians?" If that tactic doesn't subdue the querulous, a more defensive gambit can be tried: "How much more relevant is the Christian attorney or bookkeeper?" ... "If you become the so-called intelligent layman serving a State Department outpost in Mexico City, how relevant are the cocktail parties and the routine of protocol? Are they any more relevant than the Thursday evening meeting of the Christian Education Committee of the local church?" If this line doesn't get anywhere, spokesmen for the church can turn on the seminarian the full treatment of baroque piety: "The noble things of the Spirit, the uplifting influence of character, the sacred means of Grace, the majestic worship of God: are not these eternal values of unending relevance?" These debating tactics will not work; the restless seminarian has doubts which go too deep. It is true, unfortunately, that some seekers of relevance are disguising a lack of faith and nerve. In that case their questioning is more a confession than a challenge. There is no honest reason for attempting to make relevant a faith which seems false.

But if the questioner is committed to Christ, the question is both honest and poignant. It is also misstated. What he is really saying is, "I go this way but once, and I want desperately to find that form of vocational service for Christ which will, in any degree, bring life's irrelevancies into touch with Christ's relevance. Is the church the place to do it?"

Having brought the discussion to this point, the apol-
ogist for the church may clear his throat and declare,
suddenly seeing a way through the impasse, "It is not relevance, my friends, but communication—there's the rub."
That is a valid rejoinder. All of us suffer from the haze of
history. We romanticize past eras of Christian history, making them seem more "relevant" than they were. There has
probably been no time in the Christian history when sensitive Christians were not excruciatingly bothered with the
problem of "relevance" of the faith. The basic and obvious
contention, then, is that the gospel is as relevant today as
it was at any time in the past. And the Christian community is part of the gospel. In the light of this logic, what
seems to be bothering the seminarian is not really a desire
to escape institutional Christianity so much as a frantic
worry as to the effectiveness of this or that contemporary
form of the community. Thus he certainly is looking for
more communicable forms and symbols of the faith: fresh
forms of worship and preaching, livelier types of organization, any Revised Standard Version of Christianity that will
be heard, be persuasive, get to personal and social power
centers, from the human soul on out. The Christian gospel
is relevant enough, and it is our portion to translate it so
that men understand, doing with as much passion and
imagination in our time what Wesley or Augustine did in
theirs with the same gospel and to a world every bit as
stiff-necked. Considering how much we know about the
use of language, the dynamics of learning, the intricacies
of the human personality, why should we not be more excited than depressed by the task of communicating the
relevance of the gospel to our fellow pilgrims in life?

Well and good, but not quite all! Christopher Martin,

an Anglican writing in *Prism,* puts us back on the hook with his insistence that better communication without creativity will get us nowhere:

People in the Church know that it cuts little ice, so they talk about the problem of communication. If only, they cry, we could get these people to see how their responding to God through the Church is the one way to make sense of lives! So they set about devising improved means of communication ... the liturgical movement ... the ecumenical movement. ...

The weakness of this approach is that it puts persuading before showing, *didache* before *kerygma*. ... Is there not a danger that by concentrating on passing a message, and no longer seeing creation as the prime task, the Church will soon be indistinguishable from a loose assortment of nice people with vaguely good intentions towards their fellows? For to ignore creation is to deny God. To pretend that the celebrating of Holy Communion is chiefly a convenient ritual for arousing devotion, perhaps for attracting occasional doubters, is to blaspheme. The Christian religion is about life, about creating. If its rites express more than *bonhomie,* with a dash of mystery, they express this.[1]

Martin then makes an intriguing comparison with the task of the creative artist, in a passage of immense importance for understanding in what ways we may or may not make the church relevant:

Now consider what contemporary artists do, and in almost every branch you will find them desperately concerned with creating, even at the expense of persuasion, of communicating ... modern Italian painters stop being avant-garde for the fun of it, and instead investigate anew with great urgency the creative possibilities of line and color ... *in short, they want to create while the Church tries to communicate.*[2]

Martin, incidentally, puts his finger on a danger which a few of the more thoughtful seminarians recognize: that all the so-called "renewal" schemes for the church had better be more than exotic gimmicks, churchly beatnikism on display, advertising lures simply to increase attendance. In sum, if our experimenting with new forms for the church is only a form of getting people together to hear and participate in the bland version of the acculturized gospel, then what have we gained? [3]

Any Abraham desiring to lead an hegira of seminarians into our cultural wilderness need only to appear in chapel and make the following announcement to the students: "The Department of Home Missions has set aside a substantial sum of free money, gambling money, not tied to any of the usual forms of church parish subsidy. I have come here to recruit the more adventuresome among you. The church, recognizing your restlessness with the tried but not so true, now puts a challenge to you. The challenge is to commit yourself for five years to any new program about which we (an advisory committee of churchmen and seminarians) agree should be attempted, within our financial means to do so. The obligation involved is that you seriously and soberly work at the program, evaluate it, and share in the ups and downs of the team play. What would you like to do? Start a lay center . . . experiment with new forms of urban church organization . . . disorganize suburbia . . . begin a quasi-monastic order? Whatever it is, and if reasonably venturesome men can agree that it should be risked, why, take two or three companions and put your hands to the plow. The church will underwrite you on a basis of genteel poverty."

The Pied Piper would be awed at the length of the pro-

cession that would form! There is a dearth, almost a vac-
uum, of this type of gambling among the denominations.
At this writing there is a heartening word that the National
Council of Churches is seriously considering the subsidiz-
ing of a Department devoted to this type of adventuresome
planning. It should be called the Department of Ecclesiastical Wild Life, an interdenominational think-tank whose
only purpose would be to gather ideas and programatic
suggestions about the frontiers of church life. It would
work closely with seminarians and the younger clergy who
have schemes wild, hopes woolly, strategies and experiments wonderful: a place where the thin line between the
pioneering and the nutty can be drawn in comfort, where
new causes and old discontents can be bounced off one
another. Such a Department need not implement such
ideas. It could sift them, reshape them, and then say to the
denominations, "Why not try this for size?" It would be
more than a safety valve for steamy impatience; it would
be the church's recognition that just as is true of any university or industry, it must have a department of subsidized
revolutions where creative persons can get a hearing within
the established structures of church life, without waiting
for years to get into a position of authority.

The church is growing and vital when it is yeasty with
plots and cabals, with wild hopes and Young Turks, with
ecclesiological Roman candles. The church is strong when
it can undergird and surround . . . not smother . . such zip
and zest with its organizational structure. The trouble is,
of course, that top echelon church administrators, whose
burdens are heavy, are apt to interpret the "yeast" as a
threat or as an interruption. These administrators, be it

said to their understanding, must also live with plots and cabals of a petty and personality sort. Nevertheless . . . !

Here is a proposal which, hopefully, deserves a fair hearing not only by national denominations and councils of churches but by local councils and individual congregations: A local church could set aside a budget item with which to engage a lively seminarian and say to him, "Hang your coat and hat in our church, if you will; in any event, feel free to use it as a storm shelter when things go badly, but your main task is to look around our community with open eye and impressionistic gaze and devise a new type of ministry, without primary regard to membership in or genuflecting to our regular parish structure. You are free . . . we ask for no *quid pro quo*. We will help, if asked; we will become involved, if you need us. The town lies before you. Your pay check is guaranteed, now go to it!"

Should a metropolitan council of churches see virtue in this evangelical gambling, the variety of possible ministries would be multiplied and the ecumenical implication would be rewarding. Who would put a limit to the effects on Christian unity were we (the run-of-the-road denominationalists) to free younger clergy for pioneer work in Christian witness?

Finally, if the current rage for relevance reflects a genuine desire to get about the work of the People of God in our time with flair and imagination, it can only be praised. But (and on this count too many seminarians are bound to plead guilty) if much talk about relevance is double-talk, or filibuster, a mere stalling tactic by which not *angry* but *frightened* young men refuse the call to Macedonia, then it will not be the first time in Christian history that sophisticated verbosity became a form of apostasy. Even a cursory skimming of this book will reveal that in most issues the author is on the side of the seminarian; but it must be reported that on this matter of "relevance," and in the attitudes which lie behind it, far too many seminarians are just plain quitters. That harsh verdict is ventured because so many of the Relevance-Talkers seem to be tired cynics. More charitably put, the Christian ministry calls for a maturity which can combine experience and innocence without becoming disillusioned or jaded. MacNeile Dixon understood this when he wrote, "You remember how, at the opening of Goethe's Faust, Mephistophel, being stale himself, found the world stale, and reported it as such to the Almighty. The archangels took no notice of him and continued to sing of eternal freshness."

Those who have a right to talk of relevance are only those who, knowing that Eden is closed and all men sinners, yet find Creation good, God alive, and work to be done.

II. Seminarians and the Seminaries

"A low standard up there for ten years may corrupt half the parishes in the kingdom."

"That's true," said Tom, "but..."

"Yes; and so one has a right to be jealous for Oxford. Every Englishman ought to be."

Tom Brown at Oxford

6.

When things go badly in the life of the church, and when we are at wit's end, there is some relief at hand: blame the seminaries. This we do, making of the seminary the ultimate source of all mischief (and good). A logic which is, of course, as unfair to the seminaries as it is to the Holy Spirit! Seminaries may take some comfort from this in that such scapegoatism implies that we at least feel that the seminaries are important. The typical scapegoating refrain runs about as follows: seminaries manufacture ministers, ministers are supposed to know it all, and since seminaries are always begging for money, why shouldn't they be blamed for the terrible situation in Christendom? Was last Sunday's sermon only sentimental mush? Then fire the seminary homiletics professor. Doesn't the minister know how to reduce racial tensions? Discharge the Social

Ethics Department. Won't the local church budget balance? Then why doesn't the seminary have a course on church management?

We are aware that few churches can rise higher than the level of the theological education behind them—a fact which makes the atrociously poor financial support of seminaries a matter of scandal. The centrality of theological education for the health of the church makes the schools the objects of massive lobbying interests. Christian education, missions, theology, ecumenics: these and all other areas of the seminary's discipline can find long lines of special pleaders among faculty, alumni, and the church establishments. No one who is out of touch with seminaries can accurately gauge the present and future vigor of the church. These schools are the source documents for any biography of any denomination. They are in themselves objects of loyalty and criticism by the successive generations of clergy who have received their diplomas from them.

What are some of the more interesting and significant matters under discussion, pro and con, by such seminarians today, as they talk about their seminaries?

The first and most striking generalization is that the graduate student of theology very quickly feels, especially if he is studying in a university, that he is *unus contra mundum* in a way which is not true of "secular" graduate students. In short, the seminarian carries certain "plus" burdens which do not so necessarily characterize all other types of graduate students. A sympathetic understanding of seminarians cannot be gained without an appreciation of these "plus" factors.

Plus the church. The church cannot be relegated by the

seminarian to the same arm's-length distance, with the "We'll worry about that later" attitude, that is found among law students thinking about the bar association, or among medical students turning an eye occasionally toward the American Medical Association. The church is part of the gospel. As an institution it makes the deepest kind of personal claims on the seminarian. His very self-image is largely determined by it. No amount of book work or intellectual exercise will insulate the seminarian from the claims of the church. There is no division between academic purism on the one hand and discipleship in the Christian community on the other. The doctoral student in French, burrowing through the writing of Racine, need give only the most peripheral attention to the structure of the American Association of University Professors. And most surely he need not apply ontological terminology to the French department! Nor does he labor, therefore, under the extra burden of the seminary student who, although he wistfully would welcome nothing more than a chance to study without the church in the background, finds that there is no escape.

Plus God as the subject of study and the object of faith. How does one coolly study God while possessed by him? At 9:10 the attributes of God will be categorized in Lecture Room 9 by Professor Prolegomenon. At 10:10 in the Chapel there will be celebrated the Service of Holy Communion. One moment the seminarian is sorting out Isaiahs; the next he is crying out, "Holy, Holy, Holy."

True, it is equally impossible for an atheist or an agnostic doing a dissertation on "Kant's *Critique of Pure Reason*" cleanly to separate conclusions from assumptions. The seminary student, however, finds his dilemmas more

painful, more of a strain on honesty, as he attempts to
think clearly about the very God in whom he believes so
personally. Without for a moment asking for special favors,
the theological student may at least be pardoned a wistful
look at other disciplines where, though the scholars may
be criticized for the shape of their thoughts, they are not
simultaneously held to account by a watchful world's demand that conviction be matched by personal devotion
and public performance.

The ambivalence is that between thought and belief,
the difference is that between membership in an ideological
camp and discipleship in the Christian community. Unless
one is a fundamentalist or an ultrapietist, it is impossible
neatly to separate the God to whom one prays and the
God about whom one reasons. It is also impossible to anticipate what the effect of study will be on one's faith. Professor James Gustafson has put the tension in just the
right perspective by illustrating with this quotation from
Kierkegaard: "Imagine a lover who has received a letter
from his beloved. I assume that God's Word is just as precious to you as that letter is to the lover. I assume that you
read and that you think you ought to read God's Word
in the same way as the lover reads that letter." [1] Gustafson
then asks the questions which, analogously, represent the
tightrope situation of the seminarian as graduate student
and as man of faith. "Is S.K. correct? Is he totally incorrect?
Does critical study affect the passion of the love letter?
Does the passionate reading of the love letter enable us
to see what is really there? Or does it blind us to what is
there?"

Do not pity the seminarian that he must grapple with
this tension; but out of fairness to him, remember that

such is his constant situation. This plus factor can be described from another angle of vision: that of the student in the search of faith.

The medical student at his rounds or the Ph.D. candidate in English is not necessarily concerned with the quest for personal faith. But the book ends on the desk of the seminarian include a Commentary on Colossians *and* the usual "Guide to Thesis Writing." The quest for a fuller faith is not carried on in a state of controlled schizophrenia, neatly dividing faith from study. Seminary is a time when honest faith and honest doubt are inseparable. It is also a time when acute self-consciousness about such matters reaches its height. How much easier it would be if the student could *simply* study the German Reformation or the Oxford Movement or Baillie's christology without any concern for personal involvement in the problems raised. It cannot be.

The contemporary seminarian is in his quest for faith, moreover, beset by a constellation of intellectual problems which, taken together, *probably are the most disturbing set of issues to circle round the heads of seminarians since the impact of German scholarship in the nineteenth century*—an assertion made in the cool of the day and after much sampling of the evidence.

In the preface to this book many of the theological and ecclesiastical problems which test the faith and stability of the seminarian are listed. This book is not written as a treatise in any one of these problem areas, the main purpose of this writing being that of briefly indicating the scope of some of these issues. With that caveat, let us take a brief look at one of the major and violently disturbing controversies besetting all seminarians in search of faith:

the baffling questions of biblical interpretation having to do with "history, myth, kerygma, demythologizing," and related matters. Think only of the differences between Barth, Bultmann, Bornkamm, and Buri to see the exquisite tortures of contemporary hermeneutics for the seminarian. "German Sinais thunder, and Americans tremble still!" In any event, biblical studies are unbelievably volcanic and volatile. One of the key questions is to what extent the historicity of the entire New Testament is able to be vindicated in the face of modern world views and the scientific understanding of human nature. In 1955 Kummel listed the debate about the historicity of Jesus as the main controversy in the field of German New Testament research.[2] Most surely the quest for the historical Jesus has been revived in a manner which is unbelievably complex and commensurately confusing. *The final and absolutely basic issues for the seminarian qua scholar must be in New Testament scholarship, particularly as it relates to christology.* And there can be no doubt that the deadly seriousness of the present controversies in hermeneutics relating to the historicity of Jesus has caused and should cause a major crisis among seminarians. What is avant-garde in the church is often regarded as banal among seminarians; but there is no disposition to be clever or sophisticated about these basic issues in biblical theology.

The situation is complicated by the vogue of existential terminology applied to biblical interpretation. Is, for example, the New Testament to be looked upon primarily as a "superb insight into the existential plight of man," regardless of the historical validity of the key events and claims? Or, to what extent can the truth claims of the gospel be upheld in a pedagogy which talks about the "symbolic modes of man's authentic existence as portrayed in New Testament myth"? The air is full of slippery gospels, of redemptive events floating in an ectoplasmic vocabulary replete with words such as "mythopoetic . . . demythologizing . . . symbolic." It is difficult to overemphasize the anxiety this radical hermeneutics is creating among seminarians. It must be clearly understood that the anxious reaction is not the old-fashioned "What's happened to the simple gospel?" sort of thing. It is a feeling in one's bones that there are certain logical consequences in this approach to an understanding of the Bible which may undercut the evangelistic commitment. Professor Paul J. Achtemeier poses the matter in these words:

We have, in short, the anomalous fact that the new quest for the historical Jesus [referring primarily to Fuchs, Ebeling, Cullman, Bultmann, and others] by a group of men who would have to regard any valid historical fact about Jesus of Nazareth as threatening the purity of the Christian faith . . . coupled with a view of faith which denies for faith any ultimate significance in "accidental historical truths," and which finds the enduring significance of Jesus of Nazareth in the preaching about Him, the hearing of which opens for the hearer the possibility of *authentic existence*. [Italics mine] [3]

Is it, from the seminarian's point of view, possible to become a parish minister on the basis of such a christology, which makes of existential result a sufficient substitute for historical causes? Amos Wilder, with typical insight, has clarified matters by comparing the new modes of hermeneutics with nonrepresentational and surrealistic art forms.[4] That is to say, the apparent purpose of the latest and most sophisticated New Testament criticism is, in a mood of "passionate subjectivity," to have an existential encounter

(dreadful phrase) with the authentic source of New Testament power and creativity, Jesus. History is seen dynam-
ically "as dialogue and conflict, epiphany and drama."

In the plainest possible English, and at the risk of Philis-
tinism, it must be said that such biblical criticism radically
changes the meaning of the words "history" and "historical
event." An existential and dynamic search for the Jesus
of History undoubtedly uncovers the power and the saving
impact of his person in much the same way Monet's "Gare
St. Lazare" reveals dimensions about railroad stations that
a photograph of the engines would not do. But all Christians must have a more realistic understanding of the
historical events behind that faith of the early church than
the partial understanding offered us by this school of
biblical criticism. The faith of the early church cannot be
most adequately understood in terms of "existential symbols." One does, as Achtemeier implies, have the uneasy
feeling that the historical vertebra is being cut out of the
gospel, and that the Body of Christ is collapsing into a
gelatinous docetism. The understatement of the year is
Dean Samuel Miller's, ". . . the air is full of theological
embarrassment."

The exciting advances in historiography and in form-
criticism warrant a severe criticism of many of our former
ideas as to what is historical. Because of that, Professor
James Barr, of Princeton Theological Seminary, has in
his inaugural address [5] upon assuming there the Chair of
Old Testament, justly criticized such naïveté; but he
reminds us

"that I am not trying to get rid of the idea of revelation
through history. This idea is, I believe, a fair expression of a
really important element in the Bible; there really is a *Heils-*

geschichte, a series of events set within the plan of human life and in historical sequence, through which God has specially revealed himself."

The hermeneutical situation has aided a tendency to "talk around" the central issues, often in a very sophisticated way. (In all candor it must be said that this situation often goes beyond mere dispassionate analysis of scholars to an ugly form of theological cowardice.) Some veteran seminary teachers conjecture that what is happening in part is that the Ph.D. type of vocabulary and stance is filtering down to the B.D. level. Graduate students of religion are capable of talking learnedly and endlessly about the problems of Christianity, without the obligation to take an evangelical position. The B.D. students find this an attractive ground to occupy.

Seminarians and those more *au courant* with contemporary biblical scholarship remark over and again that when it comes to the Incarnation and Resurrection there seems to be either a complete failure of intelligible communication or a conspiracy of silence. Bultmannian hermeneutics is again the protagonist—or the whipping boy. For Bultmann the Incarnation and the Resurrection seem always to be held at arm's length. As one critic has noted, "For Bultmann the Resurrection is Christ in us . . . in preaching on the Incarnation and Resurrection, therefore, it appears that he demythologizes, not by fighting the mythology, but by ignoring it." [6]

One distinguished New Testament scholar, in personal conversation with the author, portrayed the dishonesty in much of the demythologizing hermeneutics as being like a skier shooting down a slope toward the abyss, but turning aside at the very last moment . . . not because of the momentum of his logic but because of fear of the consequences.[7] There is nothing new in a biblical interpretation which demands that we retranslate first-century cosmology and thought patterns. It is the most serious possible matter, however, when the basic historicity of the central claims of Christianity is the object of radical skepticism. Not all the existentialist contributions to self-understanding, nor the good works of the church, will suffice to preserve an evangelical ministry if there is not the basic faith in the God revealed in Jesus Christ, testified to in the unique events of the New Testament, particularly the Crucifixion-Resurrection narrative. The confusion is only compounded when the Bultmannites claim that they are striving for the basic christological facts!

Add to this confusion in crucial matters of biblical interpretation the related critique of linguistic analysis with its distrust of theological language; add also the fact that the theological situation in seminaries today is, at the best, wide open and, at the worst, characterized by a lack of precision. In contrast to the days or to the places in which Barthianism or fundamentalism or liberalism was dominant and well defined, there are now no sharply delineated and all-compelling theological traditions. That it is a heady time to be a theologican or a biblical scholar no one will deny! That the seminarian scarcely knows which direction to look for a favoring wind is equally obvious. As in Beckett's plays, seminarians often resemble those anonymous characters who pop their heads out of garbage cans to see who or Who is coming next. Continuing that figure, the air of wistful hope in the audience is haunted by the nagging conviction that there are absolutely basic

Who Is There?

Christian affirmations which call for clear and powerful expression. The faculty in the box seats are themselves involved in all this, turning to one another and exclaiming, "Why, I thought you were on stage next." [8] The drama critic may well write in tomorrow's column, "Unless the major theme is well acted and well supported by first-rate stars who can speak intelligibly, the audience will dribble away during the intermission."

7.

BEYOND THE MOAT

In the course of his graduate education the seminary student must leave his walled enclosure, cross the moat, and enter the jousting tournaments of the world. This is also known as field work. Everyone believes that Something Must Be Done to prepare the seminarian for the naughty world. No one is quite sure how this is to be accomplished. More time, money, and energy are wasted on these Rover Boys Abroad activities than in any other realm of seminary life. The trouble comes from two sources. First, since scholarship funds are in short supply, financial self-support often involves a field-work position taken primarily as a money-making device rather than an educational one. Years ago Professor Hugh Hartshorne of Yale Divinity School despairingly remarked that the ideal situation is for the seminary to have enough financial strength (1) to dismiss any student (no matter how affluent or pious) who doesn't meet the most rigorous academic standards and (2) to engage only in that field work which makes a genuinely solid contribution to preparation for the ministry and which can be kept in balance with other three-year B.D. objectives.

Alas, it is an imperfect world, and Dr. Hartshorne's ideal is light years away. Nevertheless, what transpires at many seminaries in the name of field work would never be tolerated at first-class schools of law or medicine. The fellowship subventions and governmental aid programs available to graduate students in nontheological fields only permit a growing contrast in field-work standards.

The grousing and the grumbling about field work is endemic among both students and faculty. Who wants to see seminarian Smith, with three precious years of formal preparation for ordination, spend most of his free time teaching the fast break to the boys' club basketball team? More appalling and inexcusable are those church-*cum*-seminary schemes which send men into regular parish positions during seminary years. The church officials clutch for these bodies, like ladies in a bargain basement, in order "to keep the small churches alive." The half-cooked pastor consequently leaves the campus on a Friday noon and returns Monday noon, exhausted by good works, remiss in his studies, and filled to the overflowing with guilt-feeling for work poorly done in each locale. The economy of Christendom is not well served by such tactics. The time given to keeping marginal churches going, or to earning cash in secular employment, will act like Gresham's law by driving out good money with bad.

Complicating the field-work issue, as it complicates everything else, is student marriage. With the faculty taking the chorus, let's all join in the singing of "What Shall We Do with the Married Students?"—who now compose about 60 per cent of graduate students. Further, if their theology is as fertile as their family lives, the church will soon be engulfed in its greatest period of creativity. The number of children is beyond count, with diapers waving in the wind. No student complaint here! Bravo. Just bills and babies, and wives teaching fourth grade. In any event, the financing of theological education becomes more burdensome, and the types of field-work positions taken by married men necessarily detract more and more time from study. Unless a married student has the wherewithal to finance his education, he is cheating himself and the church. An additional touch of asperity may be noted in this off-stage harangue, because of the increasing costs of fellowship support for family men. If early marriage is here to stay, surely it is in order to hope that the couples will postpone parenthood. One cannot also help wondering how adventuresome and pioneering a young minister is going to be when he leaves seminary with his personal library occupying one-sixth of the moving van while the play pen, crib, and the Spock baby books take the other five-sixths.

Another bemusing dimension of field work and practical preparation for the work of the parish is best introduced by the following comment of Dean Feilding of Trinity College, University of Toronto, who recently had an opportunity of observing the field-work program at a major American seminary:

Beyond the Moat

The students are unwittingly encouraged ... to have false ideas of the parish. We have been familiar for years with the seminary graduate who wants to turn his parish into nothing so much as a kind of seminary with himself cast as his favorite professor. ... I would like to see students helped more to accept the situation in the world and in the churches as it is, and to behave in that situation with the charity and understanding that is demanded of any man who believes himself called to improve it. ... Students who are now comparing their parishes and ministers unfavorably with the parishes of their imaginations and their favorite professors can all too easily become harsh utopians unable to love sinners, including of course themselves. This puts as sharply as I can what seems to me the major spiritual challenge that pastoral training must always meet.[1]

That observation has been seconded by Professor Wayne Oates, Southern Baptist Theological Seminary, Louisville, in a paper entitled, "The Seminary Professor as Bishop." He describes the attachment, in some instances almost a fixation, which many seminarians develop for particular teachers, relying on them heavily in postseminary years for advice and spiritual sustenance. This is natural enough. But one notes how subtly this type of relationship makes it more difficult for the young minister to stand alone, and how the seminarian mistakenly transfers to his first parish the same expectation of response and regard which he himself found during seminary: that is, why am I not regarded as respectfully by my parishioners as I regarded Professor Apotheosis while I was a student? Town is not gown, and seminarians must be disabused of tendencies to regard the local congregation as a lay seminary.

The tendency of the young clergyman to transfer the

roles of teacher and student from the seminary, where he was the student, to the congregation, whose members then become *his* students, may cripple the essential nature of the pastoral relationship. The young pastor becomes frustrated because the parishioners do not respond with alacrity and deference, as if the gospel were a homework assignment and the eschaton a final exam. If this is the hidden assumption of the pastor, he may tend to think of the "O.K." layman as the person who is on his way to becoming a junior clergyman. This is the same dubious assumption which may be behind the mountain of books now being written for "the intelligent layman"! The clergyman's role as servant and pastor to a revitalized laity must be understood in much more mature and realistic terms than the homogenized type of community prevailing in a seminary.

8.

REVEREND DOCTORS

A clearly observable sign of the time is the escalating of academic standards in American education. The air of expectation is higher. At the better colleges seniors today are as well educated as many of yesterday's graduate students. The competent students begrudge graduate study which is no more demanding or enlightening than what they had as undergraduates. This is just as true in theological graduate studies as in any other field. One cannot be close to seminarians and seminaries without hearing the cries and laments caused when very good students collide with outmoded and overrated seminary curriculums and expectations. This is not a generalization which covers all seminaries; but it is widespread enough, in any event.

The seminary student comes looking for a graduate school. Too often he finds the classroom routine and teaching rote which he left behind after the sophomore year in college. He also may have had the advantage in college of advanced placement or honors work—much more likely today than only ten years ago. He wants nothing to do with the "fluff and the fooling around," the "fun, fellowship, and ceramics" sort of thing which is all right at summer camps but not at graduate school. No second-rate seminary will long be able to fool the best of today's college graduates. And how the word gets around and back to the campuses!

Seminaries which are not affiliated with or located near high-caliber universities and colleges are at a serious disadvantage in meeting the educational challenges of this generation of seminarians. It is much more difficult to maintain an exemplary graduate student curriculum and ethos without such supportive and critical environment.

As student pressures, faculty standards, and church needs form their converging pressures on the curriculum several trends emerge. There is a movement toward more independent study, less classroom hopping about. The seminaries probably will settle for fewer courses per semester in order to give the students a chance for more intensive, honors-type work.[1] There is afoot a serious reconsideration of the place of biblical languages, both in terms of requirements and in the methodology of teaching language. There is a more realistic appreciation of the first-year student's demand for courses which get him to the heart-of-the-matter: theology and Bible particularly. The fact is that more and more students are being recruited first for seminary and second for ordination. This means that the first-year men must not be sidetracked into peripheral or overspecialized courses. The ideal first-year situation, which takes into account the attitudes of increasing numbers of students, is not more than three courses: all in solid biblical, theological, historical, or ethical fields. This leaves ample time for reading and for the individual counseling which is so necessary. The seminaries will hang themselves if they insist on too much the first year. If a man decides to continue, he can then be expected to meet the basic professional prerequisites. This proposal is advanced in a context of the need, as will be noted, for a four-year degree program. Obviously, an underlying assumption in what is being said is that *the first year of seminary is now a recruiting year as well as an educational year*.

Theological education ought to be the last to make any concessions to mass teaching and large classes, however much seminary treasurers, with their red ink, may wish to inflict the big-class system. Seminaries reflect the worship services of Protestantism in that there is a temptation for teachers to be wordy and preachy and desirous of much lecturing. Preparation for the ministry simply cannot be a matter of impersonal graduate study. There must be small-group work, individual attention. The seminaries need to emphasize the fact that the intellectual and the spiritual can go hand in hand only in an educational system which is geared to the individual. It is difficult to find the precise equilibrium between size and quality. The very best seminaries, academically, often are too large; and the smaller seminaries have trouble securing the best teachers. There is an embarrassing disequilibrium.

Let us now examine the case for the four-year doctoral degree program as a prerequisite for ordination and the parish ministry. The advance of knowledge makes it impossible any longer to educate adequately within the three-year program inherited from the nineteenth century—especially when the milk is adulterated with so much suspect field work. *For valid educational reasons* and for market-place-union-card reasons (we might as well be honest about it) the four-year degree seems inevitable. Such a degree is also necessary in order to keep this profession abreast of the rising educational standards of the other professions. Incidentally, the degree given should be the Th.D. or the S.T.D., not the Ph.D., which is a research and teaching degree.

Halford Luccock, from whose abrasive wit and wisdom so many generations of Yale Divinity students profited, was fond of rasping, "If you fellows took every course in the Divinity School catalogue, it would take you eighty-four years to graduate. Please leave the carrels and get about the work of redemption!" Such righteous impatience is well taken; but the nature of American education and the complexities of our culture are such that a four-year doctoral degree is a necessary step. It would also do much to quiet the academic restlessness of parish ministers, most of whom go through a period when they feel they must come back for additional "degree" work. Such restlessness is better channeled into other forms of continuing theological education. One wistful dean has even voiced the hope that the doctoral degree will cut down on the awarding of cheap D.D. degrees as honoraria for baccalaureate sermons!

As President H. P. Van Dusen has so often remarked in other contexts, the gnostic fallacy lurks in wait at every turn of advanced-degree emphasis: the naïve assumption that somehow, sometime, somewhere, and with enough degrees and intellectual purity, the kingdom of God will appear, mortar boards and all. This fallacy, however, is the other side of the coin: namely, that all we need is piety, enthusiasm, and a desire to evangelize. As always, learning and devotion must go hand in hand. A four-year, doctoral-degree preparation for the ministry can be made to combine both elements.

Community and All That. The waiting rooms of seminary deans are frequented at clockwork intervals with "concerned" students who are bound and determined to do something about the absence of "Christian community." No theological school campus is without its monuments to those who have fallen in this periodic engagement between faculty and students. The students are resolved that *koinonia* be manifest in striking fashion. The faculty gets a collective headache in a futile endeavor to devise a strategy that will usher in an atmosphere suitable to the Acts of the Apostles.

The student handbook of Princeton Theological Seminary, perhaps in an effort to say the obvious and thus fend off student campaigning for community, carries three pages devoted to "Princeton Seminary as a Christian Community." The preamble reads:

Princeton Theological Seminary is more than a school for the preparation of pastors and teachers of the Christian church. It is a community which undertakes to order its common life in accordance with the obedience of faith in Jesus Christ our Lord. Insofar as Jesus Christ is the norm and the guide of all that happens in the life of the community, it is possible to speak of Princeton Theological Seminary as a Christian Community, and to commend the privileges and responsibilities of membership to successive generations of faculty, students, and staff. Where Jesus Christ is the Lord of Life, and is at work

among those who live together in His service, the common life
of all becomes the concern of each member of the community;
and what happens to each member of the community belongs
to the common life and the well-being of all.[2]

The handbook then outlines the responsibility of each
member of the seminary in creating community: by prayer,
discussion, common concern, trust, and so forth. It points
to a healthy academic life, common worship, social life,
and absence of divisive cliques as indices of the presence
of the community. Student discipline is also discussed
under this rubric.

If definitions of community are wanted, the Princeton
statement is as thorough as any.[3] The preamble gets to the
heart of the matter: that without common loyalty to Christ
no community can be engineered. But definitions do not
create community. Like the kingdom of God, it cannot
be taken by force or by much talk. In many schools the
whole matter might best be dropped from discussion and
agendas for a three-year cooling-off period. The entire
problem begins to collect cheap solutions. The fretting
about it is jejune, halfway between the atmosphere of a
revival meeting and a football pep talk—dated and dead.

What slowly becomes visible, however, behind much of
this talk about community is the low estate of common
worship and devotional discipline on many seminary campuses. During chapel the married men are dropping quarters into the laundromat; the faculty are revising their
footnotes; and the bulk of the student body are in the
snack bar or the library. One is reminded of the story from
Rome during the Vatican Council concerning the friction
between the Italian and the German Bishops. "Those Ger-
mans will go to heaven after death," said an Italian prelate;

"there will be two gates, one marked 'Paradise,' the other 'Das Problem' . . . they will all enter the latter."

The habit of sloppy and poorly attended public worship, and desultory private devotions where they exist in seminaries, is very much a matter for viewing with alarm. The contemporary seminarian, for all his sophistication, can dodge repentance as well as the next person. What arguments can be advanced that justify a less than vigorous and constant devotional life? Lack of time? Widespread dispersal of housing? The agony of enduring one's peers as leaders of worship? What shall we say of pronunciamentos by seminary student councils to the effect that "no form of worship can be devised which satisfies the Palestrina cult, the jazz-mass gang, the cell-groupers, the full-time haters of 19th century hymns, and the demythologizers of the Apostles' Creed"? And some sympathy, please, for missing chapel because a visiting fireman from the national denominational headquarters will be advertising the Department of Audio-Visual Aids in his morning prayers? How long, O Lord, how long the list of excuses!

There are few experiences so revealing of the future staying power and growth of a parish minister as his habits of worship and devotion; and if such habits are not cultivated during the seminary years, there is every expectation of personal bankruptcy as a pastor. Worship is the native air of those who *really* believe in God. Nothing else will cleanse, fortify, and redeem with anything near the power of worship. It is literally a *sine qua non* for the minister, for all Christians. It is a matter of downright scandal that at some seminaries only a centurion's guard of students and faculty can be found regularly at their prayers. Frederick Sontag, a highly literate Christian layman, Professor of Philosophy at the Associated Colleges at Claremont, recently spent a sabbatical at a prominent American seminary (by no means atypical) and had this to observe:

The atmosphere of a seminary strikes me as emotionally explosive, and upon reflection it is hard to see how it could be otherwise. Religion is certainly deeply involved with the emotional life, as probably no other profession is, so that everyone within those walls either is or has been deeply entangled emotionally. . . . Suddenly you are struck with the fact that the hope of the church rests upon very shaky foundations, upon the unpredictable outcome of the inner struggles of these many men. If they are successful, if they win their way through to sanity and some degree of religious resolution, then they can lead and serve others. If they lose or give up the battle within themselves, then they either leave the church, taking with them some of its best talent, or plunge frantically ahead, doing untold damage to themselves and to those to whom they are supposed to represent religion. . . . Some flee from the spiritual battle into furious overt activity.[4]

The point of the quotation is not to campaign for a psychiatrist for each seminarian but to suggest that whatever the best way to handle the total emotional needs of the students, they themselves must face up to the demands for spiritual discipline, which, hard won though it is, brings an inner strength and grace that comes in no other way. Again, Protestant seminaries have much to learn from our Roman Catholic brethren. Psychological hand wringing is a typically Protestant substitute for prayer and fasting!

9.

THE HOLY SPIRIT AND
THE MINNESOTA MULTIPHASIC

Anyone who employs a heading such as the above is going to be suspect by the testing specialists as just another die-hard dilettante trying to hide ignorance behind cheap wit. Maybe. But let's not argue that point. What we want to do here is to glance at a Baedeker which will describe the main spots of interest in this psychological scenery.

In the history of American theological education the 1950's will be designated as that decade when psychological testing for and about the ministry spread its wings and began to fly. Men and women applying for admission to seminary or seeking licensure prior to ordination not only are asked the old questions about their understanding of the Trinity, but are confronted by gimlet-eyed commit-tees who wish to know if the candidate "can live as a human, experiencing pleasure and happiness without the compulsiveness to have pleasure associated with guilt, frustration, and anger." There may be doubt about the existence of the soul; there is no doubt about the psyche.

The lead pencils of the testers are now sharpened and ready before and during the seminary years. It is only logical to assume that testing evidence will be required by pastoral supply committees of individual churches within the next generation. The testing instruments most widely used by seminaries are the Strong Vocational Aptitude, the Minnesota Multiphasic, and the new Theological School Inventory.[1]

More than sixty seminaries regularly use one or more of these instruments both as aids to admissions decisions and as guides for personal counseling. In full measure they are part of the growing ritual of psychometrics and testing so prevalent in American education. Neither the scowls of the humanists, the jaundice of the intuitionists, nor the satire of those who claim that "St. Francis would never make it" will avail to halt the testing invasion. Rare the ministerial candidate who isn't thumped and X-rayed by the testing fraternity.

The delicate science of testing is anchored empirically in the dizzying twentieth-century developments in psychodynamics. Since, hopefully, all seminarians and ministers are human, they are not exempt from this growing field of human knowledge. Any reader who would like to take a close look at the sort of thing going on in this field should read the revealing essays in the proceedings of *The Conference on Motivation for the Ministry*.

As samples of "ministerial psychologizing under glass" one finds statements such as these:

Motivation [for the ministry] may be caused by an epileptic disposition which seeks ethical control of aggression; or by an anxiety for love; or by a glorified curiosity about the human body, and the great mystery of creation; or by the need to assuage guilt toward parental figures.

What is the relation between belief and emotional disturbance? From the theological point of view it is the more the tragedy for the fact that the beliefs involved in such correlation are not really theologically sanitary and are more plausibly doctrinal distortions brought on by emotionally twisted Christian interpretations. The nontheological factors beneath the doctrinal positions of churches are already a matter of public confession in the contemporary ecumenical movement. Dr. Midlefort will not be satisfied until the doctrinal factors beneath the nontheological, emotional postures of churchmen are confessed as well. He is surely right to the extent that "orthodoxy" and "judgment" do thwart human vitality and that "faith in doctrine, laws, and customs of churches does inspire guilt feeling, depressions, and rebellion." [2]

The Theological School Inventory, the result of seven years of hard work, is the first major testing instrument developed for the ministry. Other graduate professional fields have special tests, Law, for example; but the TSI differs in that it is more searching with regard to motivation and values, rather than being primarily a device to measure educational preparedness. The purpose of TSI is "to analyze and appraise the motivational structure of persons entering theological schools . . . to provide improved means of selecting and counseling theological school students." Questions, usually short-answer type, were devised which rate the students under, among others, the following rubrics: Acceptance by Others, Leadership Expectancy,

Evangelical Witness, Social Reform, Service to Persons. A major endeavor of the test is to help the seminarian understand the nature of his "call" to the ministry, as that verb is interpreted by a representative cross section of the denominations. Here the two key categories are "Natural Leading" and "Special Leading," phrases which attempt to get away from the semantic dynamite in the word "call." "Natural Leading" is characteristic of those who see God operating in human life in indirect ways, often indistinguishable from natural causes and effects, with his will understood only in the most approximate terms. "Special Leading" encompasses those who see God rather clearly intervening in human affairs, and whose will is clearly discernible.

Psychologists are notoriously gun-shy of value judgments and normative standards. They are much more content to limit their data to descriptive analysis. The use of tests for the ministry presents a major dilemma in this regard, for, unless one is to seek only quantitative measurements of educational preparedness (like the Graduate Record Examination), no significant testing for the ministry can escape such normative criteria as "good" or "successful" (ministry). In the TSI, and in much other literature about testing clergymen, an ambiguous compromise is reached in the use of the word "effective." There is much talk about devising testing criteria for discerning "effectiveness" in the ministry. This is a normative term, and public understanding by the uninitiated would be aided if it were so confessed.

The experts are the first to insist that test scores must be consulted only in the context of supplemental information of all types, including personal interviews. Admissions committees, candidates, and—at the collegiate level—parents, reassure themselves that testing is only one factor in a decision. But there is small hope for judicious balance. The popular trend is toward mathematical and psychometric evaluation of personality and intelligence. In cases of difficult decisions—and paradoxically this is more true of the nonspecialist than of the psychologist—there is a tendency to look for some "scientific bench mark," a psychometric bingo game. The same parent who scorns "all this testing" is quick to tell the neighbors when his child gets into the seven hundred percentile on the College Boards! The seminary admissions committee and the church placement officers are displaying, and will increasingly display, the same desperate ambivalence. In spite of ourselves, we shall slowly form psychometrically based notions of the good, or successful, or effective minister.

In a paper read before the Society for the Scientific Study of Religion, Howard H. Ham, Professor of Religious Education and Psychology, The Iliff School of Theology, reveals the shape of things to come in the lives of future seminarians. Dr. Ham is discussing "Personality Correlates of Ministerial Success." He records "six personal and social characteristics of personality that can be relied upon as positive indices of ministerial success": (1) A verbal intelligence score in the highest 4 per cent of the adult population. (2) The maintenance of significant emotional distance from people. (3) Flexible personality structure. (4) Moderate allocentric (other-related) rather than too much egocentric tendency. (5) Superior marital adjustment. (6) A relatively weak ego strength. As an additional fillip for seminarians to note, Ham also indicates that "the conspicuously successful minister seems to lack a quality of discipleship in seminary that faculty members value in their better students. In contrast, the ministerial failures have, with high frequency, been the especial favorites of faculty members under whose supervision they worked. In spite of hostility feeling toward authority figures, these persons seem able to feign a docility and adoration of the authority figure that is very satisfying to the seminary professor."

Let's double back and ask Dr. Ham for his profile of a successful minister. It is this: Pastor X, with a ten-year parish stint under his belt, has had his salary increased fourfold, and the size of his church has increased proportionately. He receives about double the average salary paid in his conference. The church he serves is in the top ten per cent "by whatever objective criteria may be used": value of plant, size of congregation, budget, growth record, benevolent giving, support of missions, educational program, and so on. His people think well of him, for he is doing what his denomination and his parishioners value. "His professional activity is consistent with available and generally accepted definitions of effective professional performance in any field of comparable stature." [3] Who can keep a straight face? One shudders to think what such criteria would show if applied to any of the great saints and prophets. Even more poignantly, what shape is the church in if large numbers of its members serve as an empirical base for such a profile of success? And finally, what criteria are we going to permit in testing for the ministry? The logical impasse is that tests for the ministry must involve criteria of a normative type; otherwise we might just as well restrict ourselves to general aptitude and intelligence and mental health tests—but what criteria, and who is to decide?

Devising criteria for testing for the ministry is doubly difficult because the norms vary according to the social group making the judgment. As Fichter indicates,[4] "success" or "effectiveness" as a religious professional is gauged by one's superiors in terms of conformity to institutionally sanctioned procedures; by one's peers in terms of technical competence; by one's public according to the vague norms of popularity. Add to those three judgments the more persistent one of a man's own conscience as he looks at Christ, and what psychological alchemy can produce the correct set of criteria?

Testing brings an unavoidable burden of self-consciousness to the seminarian. The exotic vocabulary of descriptive psychology can unnerve a seminarian, who may be excused for supposing that he is reading the report of a coroner's jury. The armies of multiple-choice questions and the Rohrschachian regiments whittle away at what in less self-conscious days we were wont to describe as "the hard gemlike flame of dedication to the ministry." Hard and gemlike, indeed; what can be more disturbing to one's poise and conviction than the candor of a psychologist? It is easy to sympathize with the reaction of one new seminarian who, after a couple of hours of testing about "your image of the clergy in their cultural milieu" and "the relative priority of socio-emotional factors and rational ones in your decision to enter the ministry," threw down his pencil, shouted, "The hell with it," and stalked out.

Add to this self-consciousness a mile-high stack of literature with these actual titles: "Why I Quit the Ministry," "The Ministry in the Mirror," "Why Young Ministers Are

Leaving the Church," "An Analysis of Problems of the Role of the Minister," "Pre-testing for the Ministry," "Are Ministers Cracking Up," "Why Ministers Are Breaking Down," "Building Up Breaking Down Parsons" [5]—and we have even more reason to say to the seminarians and the younger clergy, "Easy as you go!"

There are responses to this situation which are unjustifiable to any Christian, short of obscurantism. Anti-intellectualism of the "this is ridiculous" variety is a dead end. The ministry is no more exempt than any other vocation from psychological analysis. Equally futile is objection to the exotic and specialized jargon, since all disciplines need specialized vocabularies.[6] We must admit, painful though it is, that a knowledge of psychodynamics *is* therapeutic and in the long run will do more good than harm. A cleansing of motivation, a wise use of psychodynamic insight will be of enormous usefulness to the ministry; and we who are not technically competent in these areas need to tread carefully lest satire rather than understanding be our undoing, that we sound as provincial as the weather report in the *London Times:* "Fog in channel, continent isolated."

But something more important needs to be said. It parallels the criticism for and against the mountain of religious sociologizing: namely, a cautious perspective and a sense of humor. After all, any and all religious eras and religious leaders could and should be dissected and described by the sociologists and the psychologists. That we are being likewise worked over gives us a nervousness we are not unique enough to deserve. We need to remember the fine line between descriptive and normative evaluation. The Taj Mahal is so many yards wide, is made of a certain type of stone, et cetera, et cetera; but what of its beauty and its

Testing Center

splendor? This or that minister or seminarian has sex drives, may have difficulty communicating with his father, and comes from the upper middle class. But that does not mean that he cannot be a faithful servant of Christ. If we forget the normative judgments and remain bogged down in the descriptive, we shall be like the high school student who was forever suspicious of the Greek heritage because he heard it rumored that Plato was a homosexual. There is, in other words, a givenness about the gospel and loyalty to it which is there regardless of whether its proponents or its detractors are suburban schizophrenics or gray flannel mother haters. The conclusion reached, not without reluctance and suspicion, is that the research and the instrumentalities being developed in this field must be welcomed. But we are many a light year away from the answers, and everyone related to theological education needs to be forewarned about premature ones.

10.

DENOMINATIONAL MIRRORS
AND ECUMENICAL IMAGES

The church may be compared to a great temple, like St. Peter's at Rome or St. Sophia at Constantinople. It is visible and palpable, and cannot be mistaken for any other building; it is easy to see how you can enter into it, and how you leave it. But what if the Church is more like the Parthenon? Part of it stands at Athens, part lies on the ground, pieces of it are in London, other pieces in Paris, and I have been told that Sir Charles Watson found a bit of it in somebody's rockery. Yet the Parthenon exists, it is visible and it has a unity of design and substance which is almost the most remarkable of all the works of man.[1]

THE ECUMENICAL MOVEMENT REACHES EAST CHEAM

St. Palladius, East Cheam, was crowded on Saturday, the Feast of St. Dominic, when Fr. Gregorios Kurmudgian celebrated the Liturgy according to the Armenian rite. Christians of all denominations had been invited to attend.

The East Cheam Citadel Salvation Army Band provided the music. The Epistle was read in Welsh by the Revd. Bruffydd ap Meredydd, Minister of Railway View Strict and Particular Baptist Tabernacle. A choir from the Horeb Methodist Chapel led the singing of a well-loved hymn by Charles Wesley to a new setting by the curate of St. Palladius and the Red Cherry of Wraiths Rhythm Group.

What was thought to be the Gospel was sung in a rather unusual chant by a person who some believed came along with Fr. Kurmudgian. In place of the Nicene Creed, each proclaimed his own beliefs in his own words, whilst the band quietly played "The Lost Chord."

At the offertory a collection was taken in aid of the Undenominational Mission to Finnish Lapps of Gentle Birth. There was a sudden violent outburst during the censing of the oblations. It is suggested that certain Pentecostals were overcome with the gift of tongues. The children were taken into the crypt for the remainder of the service.[2]

Gone are the days when seminarians sport an ecclesiastical varsity letter sweater, with the big P for Presbyterian or the large L for Lutheran. More and more clergy, for that matter, if sermons and liturgies were analyzed by the blindfold test, would be difficult to distinguish by denomination. The ecumenical revolution on Main Street, U.S.A., among the churches which are members of the World Council, has had an enormous impact. It has produced ministers who with a minimum of retreading would feel at home in any number of other denominations. Raccoon-coat rahrahism for the Disciples or boola-boola for the Methodists is as outdated as silent movies. But, ominously enough, the cheering section in the seminary bleachers is capable these days of only a flat whisper for the ecumenical movement. The mood with regard both to denominations and to organized ecumenicity is one of unexcited acceptance.

The case for and against denominationalism is threadbare with wear, and it need not be spread out again in these pages. The ecumenical situation, however, calls for sharp comment because it is fast-changing and because the attitudes of younger churchmen concerning the achievement of greater Christian unity are matters of crucial importance.

Two conclusions can be offered: first, the truism about the end of the romantic era in ecumenicity applies to seminarians. Second, the overriding issue among younger churchmen is not either denominationalism or ecumenicity, or their proper relationships, but the whole nature, form, and function of the church. Until this younger generation gets around and through this aggravating problem of the church itself, particularly in its static parish forms, it will not and cannot become excited by ecumenical campaigns.

What ecumenical alertness there is today among seminarians is sustained only in the face of a bold and ruthless indictment of the entire church, as described in "Two Cheers for the Parish." Only a few years ago the ecumenical frontiers were occupied by those debating comparative ecclesiologies, by those determined to rediscover their unity in Christ beyond the barriers and divisions of men. Now, among seminarians at least, it may be broadly said that the shift is from confessional to sociological issues. It is difficult to determine how much of this shift is merely restlessness and noise and how much is a more decisive change of stance. It seems correct, however, to say that to many semi-

narians and younger churchmen the ecumenical movement
is an army moving in the wrong direction, or fighting the
wrong battles, or that it appears to be an Ecumenical Committee with the wrong agenda. Ecumenical leaders need to
take careful and deep soundings of this mood, for each
generation is tempted to steer an organization, when its
turn comes to control it, in terms of outmoded maps, charts
drawn up in the days of its youth. The students will have
themselves to blame, in part, if, whatever their present
attitudes toward the ecumenical movement, they do not
contribute their share and thus deepen our common
brotherhood.

It is clear that the routine of marriage has followed upon
the excitement of the ecumenical honeymoon. The bans
were published at Amsterdam in 1948, housekeeping was
set up at Evanston in 1954. The difference is that between
a trysting place and an agenda. Amsterdam was a "rendez-
vous"; New Delhi more like "the next meeting of the
couples' club." Now it is precisely at such a moment that
the seminarians, particularly those in the Interseminary
Movement, need to have a bluff called.[3] Marriages falter
when couples fail to dovetail love and critical loyalty, routine and romance, long-range commitment with initial in-
fatuation. To continue the figure, it might have been
better if the ecumenical romance had followed the marital
folkways of India, where so many get married by arrange-
ment and *then* fall in love. The challenge to all of us who
believe in the basic reasons behind the ecumenical movement is to stay with it. The World Council of Churches and
other expressions of ecumenical endeavor point beyond
themselves to the glory of Christian unity. These endeavors
must have the day-in-day-out support, however critical, of

all members of the Church who long for a fuller manifestation of our Lord's will for unity among his disciples.

The goals of ecumenicity can be realized only by prolonged and patient perseverance, the very homework of marriage. It is encouraging to remember that the exceeding youthfulness of the World Council, for example, makes it open to suggestion, willing to learn, responsive to new leadership and ideas. This is even more true of all the ecumenical "beginnings" at the national and local level. There is a freshness and youthfulness about our ecumenical strategies which should appeal to the younger generation of churchmen, especially since this ecumenical reformation has been so close, in genesis and in staff, to the various student Christian movements. The gloomiest possible disaster for ecumenicity would be for its present leaders to close doors to the students, or for the students to forsake a movement so largely sustained by students-come-of-age. A large and highly visible percentage of the present leaders of the ecumenical movement, roughly in the 45-65 age group, came up through the ranks of the various student Christian movements, with the years of key stimulation having been the seminary or graduate study years. It now seems doubtful that this type of apostolic succession is going to repeat itself with as much vigor and inevitability.[4]

Anyone entering the walls of a seminary in 1963 will find an ecumenical world, which, from the ecumenical viewpoint, is as different from the seminary of 1943 as New York City is from a walled medieval town. The very success of the ecumenical movement in theological education often camouflages the challenges which remain. Within the last twenty years the number of seminary courses in ecumenics or directly related fields has increased

800 per cent, net gain. In 1962 eighty-five per cent of all seminaries in the AATS were giving academic credit for courses in ecumenics. There has probably been no other area of theological education which has ever had such a spectacular growth. Even more to the point, each generation of seminarians is progressively more ecumenical in its approach to theology and to polity. The old battle cries of sectarian combat are largely dissipated or, when not, have little one-to-one relation to any seminary or denomination. The divisive issues cut across the churches and seminaries. In turn, the seminary faculties are, in attitude at least, more cosmopolitan and less provincial. This is strikingly true at the nondenominational seminaries.

Finley Eversole, National Director of the Interseminary Movement, has commented: "What are the implications for the ecumenical movement that a disproportionately large percentage of ecumenical leadership comes from the interdenominational seminaries?" One implication is this: that ecumenical thought and theology has won its battles, but the denominational structures continue to hold the field in theological education. That in the year of our Lord 1963 more than three-fourths of the Protestant seminary students in the United States and Canada are in seminaries whose primary configuration is denominational is an archaism almost beyond comprehension. Let's crawl out on the limb still farther: in terms of the theological realities and the sociological situation of the church, the present form of theological education cannot even be justified for denominational reasons.[5] (There may be some who now get out their saws to go to work on the limb, but they will be church officials and not seminarians.)

Seminarians and younger clergy who still have enough

interest to poke around in the ecumenical shambles—perhaps a better figure would be the ecumenical "odds-and-ends shop" of theological education—*should have their interest aroused:*

By the Interseminary Movement. Badly in need of repairs, this movement—or its moral equivalent—must take heart and rally round. It is a level of ecumenical testimony and participation which is absolutely essential to the welfare of Christian unity. It has provided a remarkable instrument for ecumenical education and training. It cannot be left to the older generations alone to continue to wield the machetes in the creeping jungles of Christian provincialism. More exactly, if the Interseminary Movement disappears, having died either of boredom or desuetude, a major crisis is created unless and until other forms of ecumenical involvement for seminarians are created.

By the Pariah Position of Youth in the Ecumenical Movement. "I didn't go all the way to New Delhi just to get dysentery," is the way one seminarian-youth delegate expressed it. There are encouraging signs that younger churchmen want to win full plenary status in ecumenical organizations and denominational parliaments. One of the hucksteristic forms of prejudice in the business world is the "House Jew" or "House Protestant" or "House Catholic" —highly personable executives deliberately employed to lure customers of their religious persuasion. This type of reasoning is not altogether absent from the councils of Christendom with regard to laity, women, and youth. Even by New Delhi in 1961, and despite its deep rootage in the World Student Christian Federation, youth delegates still had no voting privileges in the Assembly. Such limboism with regard to youth and seminarians is self-defeating. It is as obsolete as the refusal of some churches to ordain women. The *cordon sanitaire* strategy of the ecumenical movement, its general disenfranchisement of prophetic and theologically alert young people, can only result in a loss of interest. Particularly so, now that the honeymoon is over. Already many seminarians regard the ecumenical movement as "just another office at 475 Riverside Drive, along with audio-visual aids and church pension funds."

By the Implications of the New Movements and Pressures for Church Renewal. There is much talk among seminarians about the "fringe" movements, the new experiments in church life, the new forms of Christian community, the demands of the inner city, the lay movements, and the like. It is difficult to make a coherent generalization about the significance of these stirrings for the ecumenical movement, especially when the World Council of Churches has already pioneered in some of these fields. But the marked restlessness of seminarians about the cultural situation of the church and their rising insistence that the established forms of parish structure be radically questioned cannot be any longer disregarded. All the stirrings and youth leadership in the American racial situation are also part of this syndrome. There are real and basic energies in the *potpourri* of these causes which have direct implications for the future and nature of the ecumenical movement.

By the Experimentation with "Mock World Council Assemblies." All reputable law schools conduct 'Mock Courts." This is an extension of the case-study method of teaching. There have been few such ecumenical parallels among seminaries. It is a promising technique of theological education. When done, 'twere best well done! Put a

representative group of seminarians together in a conference situation somewhat similar to those of the World
Council. Give them real Faith and Order issues to debate
and work through. What honest conclusion would Lutheran, Episcopalian, Orthodox, Presbyterian and other
seminarians reach on such a matter as intercommunion?
Of particular relevance would be seminarian debates about
the doctrine of the ministry!

By New Ecumenical Forms of Worship and Liturgy.
Emerson once wrote to Carlyle, "There is not one of us
over here but has his vest-pocket utopia." There are few
seminary communities where no tinkering with worship
goes on. What seminary is not criticizing its prayer books,
emulating Taize or South India, and generally searching
for life and refreshment in new forms of worship?

*By the Possibilities of the Roman Catholic-Protestant
Dialogue.* How much of the remarkable progress in this
field is merely fashionable, how much will last beyond
Vatican Council II, is still a question. There is no doubt
that this area is a must for the present generation of seminarians and clergy. This dialogue ought to begin among
Catholics, Orthodox, and Protestants at the level of theological education, get quickly through the back-slapping
and comparative-ecclesiology stage, and on to the real
agenda, hidden or open.

*By the Ecumenical Influence of Literature and the Fine
Arts.* We are fast coming of age here, and it is a rare seminarian, indeed, who cannot find more than he can keep up
with in articles such as "Implications for Christian Anthro-
pology of the Faulkner Novels." This area is well beyond
the preciousness of a few Ph.D. theses. A major work is
crying to be written which will describe the ecumenical

potential of the arts in transcending our provincial categories of theological talk. A Lutheran schoolteacher, a Southern Baptist theologian, and a seminarian of the Reformed Church in South Africa can find a meeting ground in Dostoevski, or Sartre, or Bach, or Durrenmatt which they might never find in a Faith and Order discussion group on "The Nature of the Church." And behold the better new forms of architecture: they spin no verbal ecclesiologies, neither do they weave eschatologies; yet what unities they create!

Other ecumenical interests and possibilities could be added. It would be discouraging beyond measure if the seminarians did not respond affirmatively to such challenges. One generation must say to another, "It's your turn now; we need your strength and your ideas. Christ's prayer for unity implies your obedience, as well as ours."

A Personal Postscript:
Ordination and Authority

BEYOND FUNCTIONALISM

ORDINATION AND OFFICE

THE CATHOLIC AND PRIESTLY ORDER

Esse, Bene Esse, et Plene Esse

Ubi Christus et Spiritus Sanctus,
Ibi Ecclesia

ON PREPARING FOR ORDINATION

There are decisive hours in which a man finds the germ of a new vocation bursting forth in him, and, seized with a passion imperious as the voice of God, he takes upon his conscience the engagement to pursue the work which is henceforth to be the end of his life.

St. Francis

Genuine spiritual authority is to be found only where the ministry of hearing, helping, bearing, and proclaiming is carried out. Every cult of personality that emphasizes the distinguished qualities, virtues, and talents of another person, even though these be of an altogether spiritual nature, is worldly and has no place in the Christian community. The desire we so often hear expressed today for "episcopal figures," "priestly men," "authoritative personalities" springs frequently enough from a spiritually sick need for the admiration of men. . . . There is nothing that so sharply contradicts such a desire as the New Testament itself in its description of a bishop (I Timothy 3). One finds there nothing whatsoever with respect to worldly charm and the brilliant attributes of a spiritual personality. The bishop is a simple, faithful man, sound in faith and life, who rightly discharges his duties to the church. His authority lies in the exercise of his ministry. In the man himself there is nothing to admire.

Dietrich Bonhoeffer *

The Bishop's charge to the candidates on the eve of ordination was always most impressive, "Tomorrow I shall say to you, 'wilt thou, wilt thou, wilt thou?'. But there will come a day to you when Another will say, 'hast thou, hast thou, hast thou?'."

Charles Gore †

* *Prisoner for God* (New York: The Macmillan Company, 1954), p. 108. Used by permission.
† *The Life of Charles Gore* (London: Wm. Heineman, 1935), p. 258.

BEYOND FUNCTIONALISM

In a recent British Broadcasting Corporation program
Dr. Alec Vidler, a priest of the Church of England, had this
to say:

> Announcer: "What you're suggesting really is that the parson
> should be more equal to his parishioners...
> Vidler: "Yes...
> Announcer: "... instead of being set up on a pedestal?
> Vidler: "Break down this clerical caste—which isn't, I mean,
> is nothing essential to traditional Christianity. The early
> Christians didn't have all this. It's something that's devel-
> oped for sociological reasons, and the time has come to
> break it." [1]

That bit of conversation is symptomatic of the curious
muddle of ideas about the meaning of ordination. Can
ordination be described in purely sociological-functional

terms, does it admit one to a caste, how equal are laity and clergy, is it essential to have a clergy, et cetera, et cetera?

The United States has more diversity of opinion about the meaning of ordination, within and without the ranks of the ordained, than any other nation. It is not the purpose of this chapter to bow to left and to right, to each and all of the main orthodoxies and heresies in this field, but to make a plea for that view of ordination which can claim a normative status in Christian history, if any can, *and* to campaign against a purely functional view of the ordained ministry. The do-it-yourself ecclesiology kits of the majority of American denominations are reaming the core of dignity and authority out of the work and mission of the ordained minister. Nothing but a functional view can be formed from the left-over sawdust.

Fortunately, history has not only a dead hand, it has a reviving spirit. American Protestantism, busy making its way in this new world and eager to escape the clutch of dead hands, jettisoned or forgot whole areas of Christian history and tradition: patristics, Orthodoxy, major themes of Roman Catholicism, large areas of church doctrine and normative theology. The reappropriation and translation of this material into our own forms can often have a re-vivifying effect, as has been evident in the field of theology during the last twenty years. The doctrine of the ministry, the ordained ministry, is now, in its turn, a late-comer, and it stands on the doors of ministers' studies as an almost unrecognizable ghost. History brings an understanding of the ordained office which results in vigor and power and confident purpose, capable of transforming "The Holy Grocery Business of Christianity" into the channel of Grace and Redemption, able to give to the ordained clergyman a truer insight into the mighty dimensions of both his function and his office. We owe much in this historical rediscovery to the heritage of Faith and Order discussions in the ecumenical movement.

A Functional View of Ordination: The Least Common Denominator. Functional is an adjective with its sleeves rolled up. It fittingly mirrors the American temper, and it aptly describes the general attitude of most Protestant churches toward ordination. Like cinderblock architecture, it goes a long way with a minimum of beauty. A functional view of ordination defines the clergyman primarily by the tasks he performs. He is what he does. Unless he can "get" it, there is nothing "given" about his role. The late Dean Willard Sperry of Harvard Divinity School was fond of indicating that in the United States we have insisted that the man dignify the office rather than permitting the office to dignify the man. Functionally conceived, ordination is the starter's gun which sends the perspiring young clergyman running about his chores. He is regarded by the church as a specialized layman, vocationally trained to do specific jobs. This is the view which slips easily into that of regarding the clergyman as an employee of the church. At its best, this functional or instrumentalist view of ordination places the clergyman in the Providence of God, no more or less than any other person or part of the church.[2] At its worst, it makes of the clergyman an odd-job man who "fills the gap at weddings and funerals."

Seminary bookstores, not insignificant indices of the state of the church's health, with noticeable improvement in the last dozen years, reflect the functional view: books on how to scrapbook prayers, titillate Rotary, index the membership, outline the sermon, organize the men, keep the women busy. There are proportionately fewer volumes which root the work and nature of the ordained ministry in that doctrine of the church which sees the ordained office as a unique repository of authority.[3] Most of the writing of this sort, reflecting substantially that view of ordination which got lost somehow in history-starved American Protestantism, has come from the other side of the Atlantic: from the pens of Thomas Torrance, Austin Farrer, Bishop Kirk, P. T. Forsyth, Daniel Jenkins, Lesslie Newbigin, and others.

Why have we been so tardy in this country in giving a sympathetic consideration to the mainstream tradition about the ordained office? There are well-known themes in our own church history which suggest the answer: our primitivistic or landmark view of church history, ignoring whole centuries and vast traditions; the voluntaristic and entrepreneurial shape of the American denomination, which made salesmen and promoters of our clergy; an anti-intellectualism which couldn't have cared less about the great theologies and ecclesiologies of the past; American egalitarianism and individualism which perverted the priesthood of all believers by making it suspect to differentiate between laity and clergy in other than functional terms. Throw in for good measure the effects of revivalism . . . "introducing that gr-e-e-a-a-t servant of the Lord, and the main speaker of the evening . . ." and the concomitant pulpiteer personality cult. The result was that by the 1920's we had evolved a most singular notion of the ordained parson, with little relation to the classical doctrines of church and clergy. The Body of Christ came to appear as an accidental gathering of an audience to hear the Rev.

Mr. Orator preside over "the Big Church with the Big Heart and the Big Crowds."

It is equally clear that within the last twenty years seminarians have been in a position to recover the riches of historic theology. Had we been quicker about reappropriating the doctrine of the ministry we would not have so much unrest and carping about the ordained ministry. This present bankruptcy, this underfed functionalism, may also account for the mood of "functional unemployment" so common among so many clergy, and so well described in these words:

The old religious interests and functions of the churches have, in the popular mind at least, receded, so that they have developed a condition of technological unemployment . . . religious leaders are disposed to diversify their traditional occupations with more worldly tasks better performed by secular agents, especially trained for the purpose . . . in Protestantism this runs the range from sports to psychoanalysis.[4]

Without a strong doctrine of the ordained ministry, it is no wonder that seminarians and clergy become anxious about their proper role and authority—no wonder that they sing the vocational blues, "Who Stole My Job Away, Who . . . ?" All of us, now beginning to grope our way out of this doctrinal waste-land, owe an immense debt, not only to the revival of theology, not only to the ecumenical movement, but particularly to the disturbers of American ecclesiological blandness, from the Mercersburg theologians to the late H. Richard Niebuhr.

The functional view of the clergy is shared in varying degree by all churches. It is a necessary but minimal view. Most American Protestant churches do not realize that almost alone among the churches of Christendom, they do not go *beyond* functionalism. There is no argument with the basic assumptions of a functional clergy. In any institution there must be designated leadership, given enough of a portfolio to get the job done. No Constantinian perversion of servanthood is thus implied—only a pragmatic realism which no lasting and effective organization can do without. But at this level alone ordination is no more extraordinary or significant than the annual election of officers by the local Community Chest.

ORDINATION AND OFFICE

In the first steps of moving beyond functional definitions we must be certain not to get entangled in the debates about episcopacy and its relation to apostolic authority, valid ordination, and the rest. Let's postpone that for a moment. There is an intermediate stage to be gained: one which is common in Christian history, with the exception of the pure functionalists, to evangelicals and catholics alike. It is presented here with the fervent hope that the functionalists may wisely call it their own.

The conviction proffered is that ordination admits one to a unique and a divinely instituted *office* in the Christian church, a position and a role which cannot be defined exhaustively by functional or pragmatic terms. The *official* view is reflected, for example, in the language of the Reformers:

In the ministry God himself appears and, as the Author of his ordinance, requires his presence to be recognised in his own institution. The ministry is a sub-ministration of God, diffused throughout all the members, while the power flows from one celestial Head.

This is a poor, wretched man ... but consider the fact that the very divine majesty lies underneath. The ministry is a gift of God.

For neither the heat or the light of the sun, nor meat and drink, is so necessary to maintain the present life, as is the apostolic pastoral office to preserve a Church in the earth.[1]

The functionalists, of course, have little alternative but to consider the quotations above as the self-inflating verbiage of men with a mistaken view of the ordained office. This is not the case. The normative view here presented has impressive historical and biblical justification. From at least the second century there is massive Christian agreement that in the Providence of God a community of his people was called forth from history, first in the Old and finally in the New Testament communities. This people is part of God's gracious act of salvation. It is, as constituted by Christ and the Holy Spirit, an inherent part of the gospel. The church is not merely a social and adventitious device to keep the streets safe for women and children, nor a means of promoting clerical pomp and circumstance. We have been given the Church, including the special ministry of the ordained. It is true that both *cleros* and *laos* refer to the whole people of God. It is *also* true that from the time of the original Apostles there has been a special office of the ministry.

... they [the circumstances of the church's origins] reveal the Ministry as of Christianity's pristine order; not a convenient addendum for practical effectiveness, but itself within the structure of what God did, integral to the whole redemptive economy wrought out through Israel and through Christianity as the spiritual Israel. The Ministry is of the substance Christ brought to the shadow; of the Second Thing, to establish which He took away the first (Hebrews 10:1-9). It was itself willed and appointed by Christ as He willed and endued the Church.[2]

This ministry is related to the original Apostles. *How* it is related is a matter of sharp division of opinion. But there is overwhelming agreement that there is to be an ordained leadership in the church, an office (we shall see that Roman Catholics, Orthodox, and others regard it as also an Order), instituted to witness to and to share representatively in the work and authority of Christ.

The ordained ministry is a gift from the hand of Christ.

This is more than an historical fact. Nothing gives to this office such weight and sanction, so clearly reveals its true nature, or so sets and holds it to its divine and enduring purpose through the changing centuries as the acknowledgment of this fact . . . the ministry is the gift to the Church of Him who came not to be ministered unto but to minister. Not unless, or until, Christ himself shall become obsolete, will this fact fail to give light and understanding upon the ministry. This foundational truth is attested unmistakably in apostolic utterances, and is the ground of authority upon which the ministry is exercised throughout the Church.[3]

Such a view of the ordained office is soberly and seriously, and with awe-fullness, anchored in a view of the Church which sees it as part of the gospel.[4] Without such a view, held sincerely and not simply as a defensive *tour de force,* clergymen will be blown away by the winds of this world.

Lesslie Newbigin, commenting on First Corinthians, gives the correct perspective:

There is a real people of God in the world, a real spiritual society, a real body of Christ, a place where the light of God really shines and the life of God really pulses, and it makes the most awful and ultimate difference conceivable whether you are inside or outside of that place.[5]

It is not strictly true to say either that the Church creates the ministry or that the ministry creates the Church, but rather to say that God calls both into being as necessary for the fulfillment of his will in history. The apostolate of the Church is the human end of the Incarnational revelation. As Jesus Christ is sent of God, the ordained minister is sent by Jesus Christ. It is an office with an inherent dignity and authority not solely definable by the individual character and abilities of any incumbent. This office is not an inherited caste, most certainly it is not a job or a secretaryship. It is a sacred calling—and here we emphasize that "sacred" is that which seeks to consecrate and redeem the secular, not that which is separated from it.

What is an office? Political analogies are partially helpful. When John F. Kennedy became the President of the United States he acquired an authority, an ethos, a dignity which he never could have or deserve simply as a competent, well-educated young man from Massachusetts. P. T. Forsyth addresses himself to this definition:

Just what does the Church mean when it uses the word "office" for the work of the ministry? In our civil society public offices are created for the purpose of governing and administration. Men are elected or appointed to fill these offices of public service, but both the existence and perpetuation of the public office depend upon the wishes of the particular society. In the Church, on the other hand, we believe that the office is of divine origin. It is given in the Church. It does not depend upon the Church either for its origin or its continuation. The New Testament teaches that the sacred office of the ministry is directly derived from the triune God, even though it is given within the fellowship of the Church. We read in I Corinthians 12, that it is God who sets the offices and ministries within the Church. In Ephesians 4, the office is also called Christ's gift to the Church, and in Acts 20, Paul is represented as stating that it is the Holy Spirit who makes men the "overseers" in the church at Ephesus. Although the Church is the sphere of divine activity, the ministry is the appointed agency of that activity. No wonder that John Calvin called the office of the ministry the most important nerve of the Church.

Although from man's point of view the office of the ministry may seem to be merely a practical necessity, it is actually much more than that. It participates in the very Holiness of God. The nature of the office cannot be exhaustively defined simply by reference to its various duties and functions.[6]

With the caricature of shorthand, it can be said that the functional view interprets ordination as admitting to a job; the normative "office" view as admitting to a given dignity and authority; the Roman Catholic view of "Order" as admitting to a unique status of being. The first is thin gruel, the third claims too much.

The office of the ministry was never forsaken by mainstream Protestantism, except for left-wing functionalist American versions. Nor did the sixteenth-century attacks on the priesthood result in a disparagement of the ministerial office, except for Anabaptists. Not even the polemical assertion of the priesthood of all believers was permitted to serve as an excuse for a merely functional view of the ministry. The Reformers attempted to cleanse and restore the office of the ministry, not to abolish it or to weaken its uniqueness. In no circumstances did they see the office as one into which a man could by himself thrust himself. Examination, call of the church, personal fitness, and the rite of ordination: all were necessary.

Both Luther and Calvin set the Ministry within the universal priesthood. There is no suggestion of an antithesis between them. No branch of Puritanism opposed the idea of a separated Ministry, yet all of them fervently proclaimed the universal priesthood. Wesley was emphatic upon the subject of the functions of the laity, but in none of his writings does he make this view the ground of anti-clerical sentiments. Any notion of discarding the idea of a separated Ministry would have been unthinkable to Wesley who lived and died a true Anglican. We assert, therefore, that far from being a dividing factor, the doctrine of the priesthood of believers, properly understood, transcends differences of function, unites them in the exercise of a priesthood which is common to all.[7]

The authority of the ordained office derives from its essentiality in the church's work of salvation. Most Protestants no longer claim an authority for a particular form of church polity. Debates of polity were waved as swords by our ancestors, but biblical scholarship no longer permits us to say that the presbyterian, or episcopal, or congregational form of government and methodology of ordination is that prescribed by Holy Writ. Bishop Lawrence of Massachusetts was fond of saying, "It is remarkable how many things have been begun in my lifetime and attributed to the twelve apostles."

Above all else, the authority of the Christian clergyman derives from the truth and cosmic significance of the gospel, the gracious Act of God in Christ. As Christian and as clergyman he cannot claim that his apprehension of the gospel covers all truth, or even that the gospel is the whole truth. Only God knows that. But the Christian's rock-bottom, mainspring motivation and source of authority is his conviction that, insofar as fallible man can know, God Almighty has most truly revealed himself in Jesus Christ. It is not an authority which the world is bound to heed, but unless the Christian sincerely believes in this God, no ecclesiastical office or kudo will add any worthwhile authority to him. Volumes, of course, have been written on the ticklish subject of Christian authority—nicely balancing off tradition, personal experience, rational epistemology, and biblical record. It is out of this discomfiting mixture that each Christian finds his own faith. Even he who accepts a Church as The Authority cannot evade making the personal decision to do so.

The clergyman, by virtue of ordination, acquires a necessary authority, unlike that of other men. He has no reason for boasting in it. It calls him to sacrificial service. It admits him to no higher rank before God or ethical superiority over other men. His office is not a merit badge earned by a B.D. degree. It most certainly is not, as Dr. Vidler underlined, a "caste." At the same time, he is not merely a well-trained layman.

As mentioned previously, American church history has badly misinterpreted the phrase "priesthood of all believers" because of the egalitarian strain in our tradition. Priesthood of all believers does not mean that the clergy are superfluous, but that there is no difference of status before God between clergy and laity. No priest should stand between God and man. No one can have faith for another. We are all priests in mediating Christ to our fellow men. It is this dimension of "priestly fellowship" that is so often missed in contemporary Protestantism and which, being lacking, confuses the issue about the ordained office. In the community of faith, *qua* faith, both clergy and laity are bound to wrestle with the Angel. Priesthood of all believers does not mean that every man is his own priest. It is a recognition of the community of faith and of the opportunity and responsibility of the believer toward his neighbor—each man is a priest to every other man—a Christ unto his neighbor. The Reformers most certainly did not, in the name of the priesthood of all believers, abolish the clerical office. They rather attempted to restore it to a more apostolic and primitive purity by insisting, as over against papal hierarchy, that Christ is the only head of the Church.

The authority of the ordained office shares in the authority of Christ. This means, therefore, that it is an authority manifesting itself in service and obedience. It is not the "pecking-order" type authority which leads to ladder climbing or to authoritarianism. The nature of the ordained office is such that no man will seek it because of any sense of magisterial power or pomp. No one should ever seek ordination for such reasons; but only because, as Roswell Barnes sets it forth, "a person should feel that he has something which is so important to him and something about which he has so much enthusiasm that he feels compelled to share it with people for whose welfare he has a concern." This excitement, this dedication, this compulsion must be matched by discipline, by education, and by the sober approval of the church before it qualifies as a sufficient motive for ordination. The trouble with formal talk about "ordination and authority" is that it risks losing sight of the more significant talk about "joy and faith and fear and trembling" as the primal forces in seeking ordination. Somewhere in his writings Rufus Jones, the Quaker Sage, describes an incident during his sophomore year at Haverford when in a mathematics class he suddenly saw the beauty of pure math, and went running over the fields after class out of the sheer exhilaration of such a vision into the intellectual life. So be it! All the churchly authority in the world is a hollow and specious and pitiable thing, indeed, if these dimensions of personal devotion and arousal are not included.

THE CATHOLIC AND
PRIESTLY ORDER

There is no attempt here to give fair and equal space to the Roman Catholic understanding of ordination to the Order of the Priesthood. It is a towering tradition in the Christian mountain range, even for those who regard it as papier-mâché. The Roman Catholic (and Orthodox) priesthood is the parental and historical source of much contemporary thought about the nature of ordination and authority. It represents the other end of the spectrum from functionalism, even though it incorporates a functional definition as a subordinate way of defining the priesthood. At one time or another the tug and appeal of the priestly Order is felt by seminarians and ministers. There break out occasional migrations of free-churchmen "going over" into priestly churches. One of the reasons for this, other than the merits of the priestly Order, is the emptiness of functional views of the ministry. One young priest, in reply to a lady parishioner who thought he was taking his vestments too seriously, said, "Madam, when I wear these robes I am 1900 years old!"

Dating at least as far back as Cyprian (200-258), the priestly Order is fixed in a hierarchical and essentially sacramental view of the Church and its authority. As Chrysostom declared in *De Sacerdotio*, "The Paraclete himself has instituted this office and chosen beings living in the flesh to fulfill the ministry of angels . . . with holy dread remember those precious stones on the priest's breastplate, that mitre, that tunic, that profound silence in the inner temple."

The Roman Catholic priest is regarded as a necessary mediator of Grace, and as the embodiment on earth of Christ's authority in earth, hell, and heaven. The Council of Trent in its catechism defines priests as "Beings higher than Angels . . . priests are no longer to be called men, nor angels, but divine beings." This ontological difference in kind is the key distinction between Office and Order. An "indelible Order" was given at ordination, so that in very being the priest was different in kind from nonordained persons. He is *Alter Christus,* surpassed in ontological stature only by the Virgin Mary and the Godhead. One Protestant writer traveling through France was astounded to hear a local Roman priest say in a sermon to his congregation, "You have three natures: body, soul, and spirit; I have a fourth, because I am a priest."

Granted the assumptions of this ecclesiology, the priest lacks neither role nor authority! The assumptions are that the priestly Order is congruent with that of Christ's ministry, that Christianity is essentially a priestly religion, that the priestly celebration of the sacraments is central, that the Church as the Body of Christ is necessary for man's redemption. The logic of the priestly church is that the priesthood may exist prior to and independent of the church. According to the Catholic Encyclopedia, "The priesthood forms so indispensable a foundation of Christianity that its removal would entail the destruction of the whole edifice." The original Apostles are, in effect, the first College of Cardinals; they created the Church, they transmitted authority to an unbroken line of episcopal successors.

Though this Roman Catholic doctrine of the priesthood does not apply, *pari passu,* to Anglicanism and other priestly churches, the essential flavor is the same. Whatever the evangelical Protestant may feel about the aptness of the priesthood as an interpretation of Christianity, he does well to study it carefully.

Episcopal Controversy. A guided tour through the quicksands of Faith and Order, as well as through the corridors of seminary discussions, will come sooner or later to a gate marked, "All Calmness Abandon, Ye Who Enter Here." It is the entry way to the great debate about the relation between ordained authority and episcopacy. The day is over when American Protestant seminarians and churchmen of the presbyterial and congregational forms can dismiss or ignore these debates as being minor matters of the law. Not only do they constitute one of the most irritating ecumenical impasses, but they raise in needle-sharp fashion the question of ordained authority.

From the pages of the Ecumenical Press Service of the World Council of Churches, December, 1962, comes this typical news item:

ANGLICAN SOCIETY OPPOSES OPEN COMMUNION

(London)—Following requests from its members for guidance on the subject of intercommunion, the Church Union (a society of Church of England members who hold to the catholic tradition of the Church) has said in a statement: "The Church Union believes that the cause of unity is not advanced by open Communion services at which members of churches not in relations of communion with the Church of England are invited to receive Holy Communion. . . ."

The statement goes on to stress communion with the bishop as the accepted mark of unity in the early Church, and schism as a state of separation from the bishop. The communion together of separated Christians who then return to their separate churches does not involve a sufficient acknowledgment of the bishop, says the statement, to establish permanent communion.

The fact of division within the Church of England over the question of intercommunion shows that, the statement says, mutual respect and understanding are called for. To regard the Holy Communion as a means to unity runs counter to catholic tradition.

In its concluding paragraph the statement urges joint worship within the context of different liturgical traditions, and maintains that "the joy of communion must wait upon the attainment of the unity which it properly reflects." [1]

The root question, when Faith and Order discussions of the doctrine of the ministry are analyzed, is this: "To what extent, if any, is the historic and/or apostolic episcopal succession a necessary sign of a valid Christian ministry?" The dimensions of the issue are outlined by John Line:

The problem of the Church's ministry is one that, in ecclesiastical discussions throughout the world, is coming more and more into the foreground. This is partly because, in the efforts of the Churches to come together, in the ecumenical movement or in plans for formal reunion, it has become apparent that it is in connection with the ministry and questions cognate to it that the chief—one could almost say all—hindrances to unity have arisen. Leaders of the churches repeatedly assert that there is nothing to keep them apart in their basic beliefs, in what they profess concerning God, Christ, and the Holy Spirit, the divine provision of Salvation, Resurrection, and the Future Life.[2]

Esse, Bene Esse, et Plene Esse

In the ecumenical free-for-all concerning the doctrine of the ministry the Roman Catholics, the Orthodox, the Anglicans, and (with varying opinions) the Scandinavian Lutherans, insist on the episcopacy. In the American scene the Episcopalians are the most intriguing because of their ambivalent attitudes toward Protestantism and because of the churchmanship differences within that communion itself. It is safe to say that no other denomination is so tempting, and withal so infuriating, to all those seminarians and Protestant clergy who have at one time or another "considered a change." The day is gone, however, when the Protestant Episcopal Church could woo the wistful by the *via media* slogan. The ecumenical reformation has effected such an "interchange of ecclesiological parts," liturgical borrowing, and theological consensus that the old "Protestant" and "Catholic" categories no longer apply with any tailor-made sureness.

Within Anglicanism there are two main views regarding the nature and efficacy of the episcopacy. The first favors what it calls *The Historic Episcopate.* Together with the faithful preaching of the Word of God, and with the Prayer Book Liturgy, it is felt that authority and continuity are best, but not necessarily, provided the Christian church by a regular and orderly progression of episcopal ordinations. This is seen as a cohesive and binding principle of organic life, granting visible unity. This party within Anglicanism is not wedded inflexibly to a belief in unbroken episcopal succession. It simply regards the existing forms of transmitting ordination as of the *bene esse* or *plene esse,* not *esse,* of the church. This group of clergy, largely depending upon the views of the diocesan Bishop, may or may not favor open communion. The most liberal wing of this school has its leading spokesmen in Bishops Stephen Neill and J. A. T. Robinson. They reject the episcopacy as of the *esse* of the Church and would not unchurch any part of the Body of Christ which has failed to preserve it.

The second party, Anglo-Catholic, tightens the screws one notch more and interprets historic episcopacy in the more inflexible terms of *Apostolic Succession.* This maintains that there is a direct and unbroken line of succession with the original apostolate maintained in church history and that it must be maintained in contemporary ordination as of the *esse* of the Church's life. In the words of Charles Gore,

... a universal spiritual society, in which the apostolic succession of the Bishops constitutes by divine appointment a visible link between different epochs, witnessing everywhere to that permanent element in human nature to which Christ's Gospel appeals ... that fundamental humanity, underlying all developments and variations, in virtue of which there becomes possible a real spiritual continuity between the generations.[1]

An Anglican hymn of the Victorian era phrases it quaintly:

His twelve Apostles first He made, His ministers of grace;
And they their hands on others laid, to fill in turn their place.
So age by age, and year by year, His grace was handed on
And still the holy church is here, although her Lord is gone.

The late Archbishop of Canterbury, William Temple, a magnificent figure of ecumenical irenicism, expressed this conviction in this way:

So when I consecrate a godly and well-learned man to the office and work of Bishop in the church of God, I do not act as a representative of the Church, if by that is meant the whole number of contemporary Christians; but I do act as the ministerial instrument of Christ in His Body the Church. The authority by which I act is His, transmitted to me through His apostles and those to whom they committed it; I hold it neither from the Church nor apart from the Church; but from Christ in the Church.[2]

The fullest exposition of the Anglo-Catholic position, as over against that of Neill and Robinson, is in *The Apostolic Ministry*, a volume built around the thesis that there is an essential self-recruiting ministry as the appointed means for maintaining the Church's unity. The episcopacy is the "glue" of the Church. Any charismatic concept of ministry is rejected in favor of the "special sphere of grace, possessed of spiritual gifts and of the power as well as the right to dispense them to others; and in no other way could he [the aspirant to ministerial office] enter that sphere." [3]

In general, if *any* generalization is possible about Anglicans (!), the motto is *Ubi Episcopus, Ibi Ecclesia*. The appeal to seminarians of other confessions seems to be a feeling that "in a way verging on mystique" the Anglican ministry has more authority.

*Ubi Christus et
Spiritus Sanctus,
Ibi Ecclesia*

The caption above is too neat, but it gives the general tone of the evangelical Protestant objection to Anglican, Roman, and Orthodox conceptions of ordination and authority. Episcopacy is not a prerequisite of valid ordination or parity of ministries, and anyone who looks to episcopacy as a major source of authority is mistaking form and substance. The Protestant must regard the logic of episcopal arguments as on a par with the logic of the white rabbit in that scene in Alice in Wonderland where the rabbit attempts to repair the watch of the Mad Hatter by smearing butter on it. When the watch still fails to tick, the rabbit runs off, muttering, "But it was the *best* butter, the very best!"

The episcopal claims also remind one of the famous interdenominational communion administered by the Bishop of Mombasa which created controversy between the ecumenicists and the purists in the Anglican Church at home until Archbishop Davidson surpassed himself in tact by suggesting that whilst the events at Kikuyu had been most pleasing in the sight of God they were not to be permitted to occur again!

Gone are the days when most Protestants can legitimately find any *jure divino* sanction for any form of polity. Indeed, as T. W. Manson has said, "Our problem is not the division of the churches, but the manifest success of many forms of polity." More importantly, the authority of the ordained minister has nothing essentially to do with either historic episcopacy or apostolic succession. True ordination and true authority come only from the "apostolicity of faithfulness to Christ." This school of thought, of course, would agree that there ought to be regular and sober ways of ordaining men to the ministry—related to the ordinand's character, faith, churchly approval, education. Antinomianism and "enthusiasm" are much distrusted. Nevertheless, this tradition stoutly maintains, episcopacy has been no more or less successful than any other form of polity in preventing heresy. The authority of the original apostolate was *sui generis;* it ended with them, and there is no mechanical way of handing it on. To claim so is to ignore the Holy Spirit in the Church as the true ambassador (*shaliach*) of God.

Writes P. T. Forsyth,

The Apostolic Succession is the evangelical succession. It is not a vertical continuity descending in a line, but a solidary, spreading throughout a mass; not a chain on which the church is hung, but a nervous system pervading it and, by the Word, continually creating it. It is more a succession of truth than of persons.[1]

To clinch this argument, evangelical scholarship maintains that it is absolutely impossible, even granting the efficacy of manual traduction of authority, to demonstrate unbroken lines of bishops going back to the first apostles. Newman's claim, for example, that "if we trace the power of ordination from hand to hand, of course we shall come to the original Apostles at last . . ."[2] is nonsense. It might (a big if) get back to Cyprian; but even so it is chronologically impossible that any contemporary of Cyprian could have been ordained by Timothy, Titus, Linus, Clement, Polycarp, the unnamed Galatian elders, or the Asian Bishops said to have been commissioned by John. There are reliable lists of successive bishops at Jerusalem, Antioch, Alexandria, and Rome; but prior to A.D. 250 not a word about their ordination.

George Bernard Shaw, more an evangelical than he realized, maintained that the only true apostolic succession was in a cannibal tribe where the retiring witch doctor was eaten by his successors!

Evangelical Protestant counsel to its seminarians concerning their ordination and authority rests ultimately, not on the act of ordination within this tradition or that, but upon the truth of Christianity in the first place, and the nature of the Church, in the second. Personal experience, church tradition, the intellectual heritage, and, above all, the testimony of Holy Scripture: these intertwine and issue

finally in that mysterious phrase, "The truth as I see it."
For the evangelical Protestant clergyman the authority of
his work and his role, the validity of his office, must go to
deeper sources than church polity.

The Act of Ordination [1] is the final step completing the call to the Christian ministry. There is justification for maintaining that the vast majority of ordination services are not given the dignity and the proper preparation which they deserve. The service should not be put together with last-minute bits of ecclesiastical paper and liturgical glue. The ordinand ought to have a clear conception of the full meaning of the service. It is a tremendous and awe-inspiring moment, not merely a formalized addendum to the B.D. degree.

Each church will have to speak for itself, but this question deserves an answer. Are your ordinands carefully and formally examined well ahead of the date of the Ordination Service? There is something flippant and shallow about an invitation to an Ordination which announces that the examination will take place at 5 P.M., the church supper at 6, and the Service of Ordination at 7—"we shall then proceed to the ordaining of...." One can smell the casserole at the very moment a benign and hungry delegation of clergy and laity are "examining" the candidate. It's about as sorry a performance as ordering a diploma from a mail-order catalogue. These perfunctory arrangements make it obvious that the examination is little more than a *pro forma* affair. The church has every right to examine, and the ordinands should be well advised as to the standards. Examinations for ordination should be held at least a month in advance, and in no case should invitations go out before the ordinand has been approved by the examining committee or chaplain.

The careful examination by the church of all candidates for ordination is a matter of the utmost gravity. There need be no concessions to sentimentality either in the examination proper or in any routine which gives the ordinand and the public the impression that the church is gladly settling for any warm body just out of seminary. It is advisable that even prior to the formal examination, the ordinand have a chance to meet with a small committee or examining chaplain in order to anticipate and correct defects. Finally, if at the public examination the ordinand cannot express himself clearly as to the central matters of the Christian faith or if, even in his clarity, it is obvious that he is not ready for ordination, no manpower need or personal affection (or the presence of watery-eyed relatives) should prevent a negative vote and a reappraisal of the situation, both with compassion and with honesty.

There is a further suggestion which may commend itself

to the reader. The nearness of ordination is the most appropriate of all times in which seminarians, particularly Protestants, need to go on a devotional retreat. Several months prior to the Service of Ordination, and under the leadership of two or three of the finest pastors, regional retreats of at least three or four days' duration should be held: a time for prayer, conversation, and a steady contemplation of the meaning of ordination. In short, a small group of ordinands, together giving sustained and urgent attention to the nature of the Church and its ordained ministry, would thus approach their individual ordination services in a preparatory frame of mind worthy of the occasion.

The final plea, and with this we close, is that the actual Service of Ordination be as ecumenical in fact as it is in theory. For all churches ordain to the "Church of Jesus Christ" and not only to an individual denomination, such as Roman Catholic or Southern Baptist. What distant battlements of The Church Universal might be more visible if in the ordination of men to the official ministry of the church we could actualize and symbolize the unity we so loudly assert we have been given by Christ, and for which he prayed. Unless there are grievous and agonizing reasons why a particular denomination will not participate in the ordination of men to the ministry of another communion, would it not be splendid and altogether fitting that services of ordination be celebrated ecumenically, including the laying on of hands?

A Service of Ordination could be devised with which many communions could agree. Why not, for example, hope that the ordaining committee in a particular Synod of the United Church of Christ would invite representatives of all neighboring Christian churches to "join with us in the ordaining of ——————— to the Christian ministry," with the clergy and/or laity of the other denominations marching in the processional and taking various sections of the Service: whether it be the prayers, or reading the Scripture, the Charge to the Congregation, or the Laying On of Hands? Then, with what magnificent justification could the whole congregation of clergy and people rise to sing *"Venite, Spiritus Sanctus"!*

A Personal Preface: From the Seminary Steps

1. *Christian Faith and the Contemporary Arts,* Finley Eversole, ed. (New York: Abingdon Press, 1957), p. 221.

1. Sociological Thunder and Cultural Lightning

1. Harold Wright in *Duke Divinity School Bulletin,* Vol. 27, No. 3, Nov., 1962, pp. 139-140. Used by permission.
2. *Making the Ministry Relevant,* Hans Hoffman, ed. (New York: Charles Scribner's Sons, 1962), p. 16.
3. From *The Noise of Solemn Assemblies* by Peter L. Berger. Copyright © 1961 by Peter L. Berger. Reprinted by permission of Doubleday & Company, Inc. Page 45.
4. *Ibid.,* p. 165.
5. Gibson Winter, *The Suburban Captivity of the Churches* (New York: Doubleday & Co., Inc., 1961), p. 165.
6. From *Protestant-Catholic-Jew* by Will Herberg. Copyright © 1955 by Will Herberg. Reprinted by permission of Doubleday & Company, Inc. Page 72.
7. In *Beyond Religion* (Philadelphia: The Westminster Press, 1962), p. 100.
8. By Alan B. Anderson, *Behold,* June, 1962, p. 11. Used by permission of the Chicago Inner City Methodist Ministers' Fellowship.
9. Having said that, the reader of these sociology books must in turn be careful not to reject out of hand the valid proposals found therein.

10. See his review of Daniel Boorstin's *The American Image* in *The Yale Review*, Jan., 1962, p. 650.
11. The headquarters, replete with banks of elevators, escalators, underground garages, etc. of the National Council of Churches and major denominational and ecumenical agencies. "475" symbolizes all that on which nineteenth-century Protestant nostalgia wishes to vent its frustrations.
12. For an intriguing presentation of how a thoughtful person reacts to large organizations, see Lewis Meizner, "Injustice and Bureaucracy," *The Yale Review*, June, 1962.
13. In a speech to the National Lutheran Student Association, 1962.

2. Suburb and Inner City: Horatio Alger and the Jesuits

1. As in *The Mackerel Plaza* (Boston: Little, Brown and Co., 1952).
2. In *Christianity and Crisis*, Nov. 26, 1962, p. 209.
3. There is hope that such a salary plan might permit the slow but calculated riddance from American Protestantism of the manse system, a hangover of nineteenth-century paternalism.

3. On Being a Professional Christian

1. John L'Heureux, in *The Yale Review*, Vol. I, March, 1961, No. 3, p. 384. © Yale University Press. Used by permission.
2. *Minister* (New York: The Macmillan Company, 1963).
3. Joseph H. Fichter, *Religion as an Occupation* (Notre Dame, Ind.: University of Notre Dame Press, 1961), p. 92. This is an excellent survey of the dimensions of religious professionalization.
4. Director's Report, AATS, April, 1959.
5. Evelyn Waugh, *The National Review*, Nov., 1962.
6. Stephen Neill, *Anglicanism* (Harmondsworth, Middlesex, Eng.: Penguin Books Ltd., 1959; and Baltimore: Penguin Books, Inc.), p. 110.
7. Roy Lewis and Angus Maude, *Professional People* (London: David Higham Associates, Ltd., 1952), p. 273.

4. Unofficial Halos: Some Enchanting Laymen

1. Hendrik Kraemer, *A Theology of the Laity,* 1958; Francis Ayres, *The Ministry of the Laity,* 1962; Arnold Come, *Agents of Reconciliation,* 1960—all three books published by The Westminster Press. Come's book seems to favor the abolition of the terminology, if not the categories, of laity and clergy. His book, which should be read for its novelty, presents a pseudo-solution. It would seem to be more effective to argue that both laity and clergy need to be accorded their full dignity. They are complementary aspects of the Christian Body, not mutually contradictory.

2. The author of this book was chairman of the Committee for New Delhi, charged by his church to select a delegation. It ended up with only one third lay! *Mea culpa.*

5. The Relevance Syndrome

1. "Our Cult and Our Culture," in *Prism,* An Anglican Monthly, Nov., 1962. Used by permission.

2. *Ibid.*

3. The ultimate in *ersatz* Christian communication is portrayed in *Big Ball of Wax* by Shepherd Mead (New York: Simon and Schuster, Inc., 1954). In this horror story a church is depicted which has launched its "wares" as a public relations and advertising campaign launches a new toothpaste—personal counseling via individualized TV, etc.—all communication, no redemption!

6. Seminarian *Plus*

1. *For Self-Examination,* Recommended for the Times, S. Kierkegaard. Translation from the Danish by Edna and Howard Hong, 1940. Used by permission of Augsburg Publishing House, Copyright Owner. Page 25.

2. In *New Testament Studies,* Feb., 1955.

3. "Is the New Quest Docetic?" *Theology Today,* Oct., 1962. Used by permission.

4. In *Christianity and Crisis,* Jan. 7, 1963.
5. Delivered Dec. 4, 1962.
6. John W. Bunting, "Demythologizing in the Pulpit," *Religion and Life,* Summer, 1962.
7. See also John Macquarrie's illustration in *Scope of Demythologizing* (London: SCM Press, 1960), p. 11.
8. Dean Walter Muelder of the Boston University School of Theology, in an address in 1962 to the AATS, made the same point in another way when he noted that theological school faculties are so engrossed in their specialties that each faculty member assumes the other is presenting the gospel.

7. Beyond the Moat

1. Dean George Feilding in an unpublished manuscript.

8. Reverend Doctors

1. Recent curricular changes at Hartford Theological Seminary and at Union Theological Seminary in New York are very much in this direction.
2. Princeton Theological Seminary *Handbook,* 1962-1963, p. 146. Used by permission.
3. *Ibid.,* pp. 146-148.
4. From *Religion in Life,* Autumn, 1962, copyright © Abingdon Press, in the article "Socrates in the Seminary" by Frederick Sontag, pp. 544f. Used by permission.

9. The Holy Spirit and the Minnesota Multiphasic

1. Developed by the Educational Testing Service under a grant from the Lilly Endowment.
2. *The Conference on Motivation for the Ministry,* Samuel Southard, ed. (Louisville, Ky.: Southern Baptist Seminary, 1959). Used by permission.
3. *Iliff Review,* Winter, 1960, pp. 3-9. It is not clear whether Prof. Ham agrees with this understanding of a successful minister or

whether he is simply repeating the prevailing opinion of church goers.

4. *Op. cit.*, p. 178. (See Note 3 in Ch. 3.)

5. Add *Bachelor of Divinity: uncertain servants in seminary and ministry!*

6. One suspects that academic gamesmanship often resorts deliberately to esoteric language as a defensive smoke-screen against common sense.

10. Denominational Mirrors and Ecumenical Images

1. John Lawrence, *The Hard Facts of Unity* (London: Student Christian Movement Press Limited, 1961), p. 11. Used by permission.

2. *Prism,* An Anglican Monthly, Jan., 1963, p. 58. Used by permission.

3. Even as this goes to press the Interseminary Movement is being radically re-examined by a Study Commission of the National Council of Churches.

4. See also J. Robert Nelson, "The Education of Homo Ecumenicus," *Ecumenical Review,* Jan., 1963; and Walter D. Wagoner, "Bent Twigs and Ecumenical Branches," *Unity in Mid-Career* (New York: The Macmillan Company, 1963).

5. There is every reason why denominations should operate seminaries. But there are no longer sufficient reasons for such schools being so top-heavy in one tradition. As a guess, 60 per cent of one denomination in either faculty or student body is plenty!

Beyond Functionalism

1. "Meeting Point Program," Nov. 4, 1962.

2. A very good outline of the instrumentalist apologia is to be found in *The Church and Its Changing Ministry,* Robert C. Johnson, ed. (Philadelphia: General Assembly of the United Presbyterian Church, 1961). See particularly pp. 40-41.

3. Keith Bridston, in a letter to the author, wrote: ". . . One of the problems of the ministry is that it is today living 'between the times' and, therefore, insecurity is unavoidable. To be a minister

today *means* being insecure about the vocation, the authority, and the relevance of the ministry in today's Church and today's world. This may be the particular cross which has to be borne by the modern minister and theological student. But even earthen vessels can carry *something* . . . and perhaps *only* earthen vessels can carry certain things. And the value of a vessel is not in itself but in what it is given to carry. Let us, therefore, have more useful 'pots' [not given to much brooding over authority] and fewer beautiful vases [given to display of clerical position]."

4. Author unknown. It has been attributed to Horace Kallen, of the New School for Social Research.

Ordination and Office

1. The indispensable book for understanding this normative view of ordination is *The Doctrines of the Ministerial Order in the Reformed Churches in the Sixteenth and Seventeenth Centuries* by James L. Ainslie (Edinburgh: T. & T. Clark, 1940).

2. John Line, *The Doctrine of the Christian Ministry* (London: Lutterworth Press, 1959), p. 128. More than any other book, this volume is closest to the views of the present writer.

3. M. Stephen James, "The Place and Authority of the Ministry in the Church," *New Brunswick Theological Seminary Bulletin,* Winter, 1957, p. 7. Used by permission.

4. "Part of the gospel" is not a felicitous phrase. "Extension of the Incarnation" is not an accurate one. Perhaps, as Claude Welch has phrased it in *The Reality of the Church* (New York: Charles Scribner's Sons, 1958), pp. 81ff., "The Being of the Church is analogous with the person of its Lord." In any case, the point here is to take with the utmost seriousness the providentially appointed nature and role of the Church.

5. From *The Household of God,* Lesslie Newbigin. Friendship Press, New York. Used by permission.

6. *Congregationalism and Reunion* (London: Independent Press, Ltd., 1952), p. 58. Used by permission.

7. Cyril Eastwood, *The Priesthood of All Believers* (London: The Epworth Press, 1960). Used by permission.

The Catholic and Priestly Order

1. Used by permission.
2. *The Doctrine of the Christian Ministry* (London: Lutterworth Press, 1959), p. 7. Used by permission.

Esse, Bene Esse, et Plene Esse

1. *The Church and the Ministry*, rev. ed. (London: S.P.C.K., 1949), Chapter VII. Used by permission.
2. *The Church Looks Forward* (London: Macmillan & Co. Ltd., 1944), p. 24. Used by permission of the publishers.
3. Kenneth Kirk, ed. (London: Hodder and Stoughton, 1946). See especially pp. 1-52.

Ubi Christus et Spiritus Sanctus, Ibi Ecclesia

1. *The Church and Sacrament* (London: Longmans, Green & Co., Ltd., 1917).
2. *Tracts for the Time*, No. 1, p. 3.

On Preparing for Ordination

1. Protestants are really not sure what to call ordination: is it a rite, a ceremony, an act of recognition—in what sense is it sacramental?